Swing Trading Strategies 2021

Complete Investing Guide For Beginners

Table of Contents

INTRODUCTION

To make informed investment decisions, you must first learn about the stock market. It would be best to choose the appropriate stocks, which necessitates a thorough understanding of its annual report and financial statements. Learn how to decipher what a stock reflects in a business and how to calculate its true worth.

It will help you make smarter investment decisions by avoiding the expensive mistake of buying a company's stock when the market has inflated the share price compared to its value.

Stock Market Terms

Knowing the terminology is the first step toward understanding the stock market. Here are a few phrases and terms that are often used:

- **Earnings per Share (EPS):** The company's net profit is divided by the number of outstanding stock shares.

- **Going Public:** Slang for a corporation preparing an initial public offering (IPO) of its stock.

- **IPO (Initial Public Offering):** When a company offers its stock for the first time, it is known as an IPO.

- **Market Cap:** Market capitalization is the amount of money you'd have to spend if you purchased every single share of a company's stock. To calculate the market capitalization, multiply the number of shares by their price.

- **Share:** A share, also known as a single common stock, is a unit of an investor's equity in a portion of a company's gains, losses, and properties. When a company carves itself into bits and sells them to investors for cash, it creates shares.

- **Ticker Symbol :** A series of letters that denotes a specific stock on the stock exchange. The Coca-Cola Company, for example, has the ticker symbol K.O., and Johnson & Johnson has the ticker symbol JNJ.

- **Underwriter:** A financial institution or investment bank that handles all of the paperwork and coordinates the business's IPO.

If you're thinking about starting swing trading, this book will help you figure out if it's right for you.

Swing trading is a common form of trading in which traders keep their positions open for longer than a day. Day trading does not permit traders to close their positions in a single day Swing traders usually target a greater portion of the market and wait for an offer for the underlying to surface. At this point, they trade in the trend's direction. Swing trading has been around for a long time. But why is that? An established trend is more permanent than swing trading but is not relatively long-term as trend trading, which can last many weeks or months. Swing trading is a middle ground between the two extremes, concentrating on profiting from short-term market fluctuations resulting from shifts in corporate fundamentals. Picking the right stocks with a propensity to rise in a short period is the secret to profiting from swing trading. Swing traders make some small wins to add to their overall profit while waiting for a greater profit to appear. It allows them to secure a higher profit margin. Swing traders do this by keeping their stop loss levels low, about 2-3 percent, and maintaining a profit-to-loss ratio of 3:1. It is done to avoid taking too many chances. A considerable loss can wipe out small gains from smaller swings. Swing traders select their stocks carefully to avoid making errors.

CHAPTER 1
Swing Trading

Swing trading is a speculative trading style commonly used in financial markets such as bonds, commodities, foreign exchange, stocks, and stock indexes. Swing trading usually necessitates a swing trader holding his or her position for more than one trading day, typically 2 to 5 trading days. Swing trading is popular in the trading world because it typically has a good risk-to-reward ratio, which means the likelihood of profit is greater than the risk involved in each trade.

Swing trading strives for a benefit probability of 100 pips in general. Any market swing has profit potential. Swing traders, particularly in the foreign exchange and stock index markets, can go long or short of taking advantage of any opportunity. It also means that if a market is volatile during a trading week, a swing trader may come across several trading opportunities. Swing trading has fewer trading opportunities than scalping or day trading, but as you can see, if you use this trading style, you will have more time to do other things because you will not have to hold your eyes on a market the whole trading day. Of course, you'll have fewer chances, but each one will have a high probability of winning. What trading style you use is entirely up to you. There are always pluses and minuses in every trading strategy.

Now, if you are positive that you want to try swing trading, you will find some strategies from a range of online tools. Swing trading books and other educational materials are available. You may also visit and participate in some trading forums. However, to warn that some swindlers take advantage of naive investors who aren't interested in advice. Only be cautious about such individuals. Swing trading has fewer trading opportunities than scalping or day trading, but as you can see, if you use this trading style, you will have more time to do other things because you will not have to hold your eyes on a market the whole trading day. Of course, you'll have fewer chances, but each one will have a high probability of winning. What trading style you use is entirely up to you. There are always pluses and minuses in every trading strategy.

Now, if you are positive that you want to try swing trading, you will find some strategies from a range of online tools. Swing trading books and other educational materials are available. You may also visit and participate in some trading forums. However, to warn that some swindlers take advantage of naive investors who aren't interested in advice. Only be cautious about such individuals. Fortunately, with some simple knowledge and experience in swing trading, you too can be a successful swing trader. Perhaps better, you can devise your swing trading strategies. Many people like to build their swing trading strategies because they are the only ones who understand their trading personality, desires, and style. Never give up on your goal of becoming an outstanding swing trader; while it will undoubtedly take more time to master swing trading, your efforts will be rewarded in the end.

The financial markets are incredibly complex, and there are several strategies for profiting from them. There is a range of trading types available in addition to the vast number of available trading strategies. The period during which you exchange is one of the essential differences in trading style.

Long-term traders are on one end of the spectrum; they seek to track long-term patterns that can last months or even years. Long-term trading has several benefits, one of which is the opportunity for significant gains. However, as in any other method of trading, there is the possibility of losing money. Following a pattern consistently for several months can usually outweigh what can be done in the short term. On the other hand, long-term trading usually does not necessitate much focus beyond a limited amount of regular monitoring. It does, however, necessitate more diligence and would undoubtedly provide fewer opportunities to trade.

Scalpers are on the other end of the continuum. Scalpers engage in ultra-short-term transactions, which can last just a few minutes, to make small profits before leaving. Scalpers are content to earn a fraction of a point here and there. The relatively short duration of these trades has one advantage: it reduces your exposure to the market. Often, since you're just searching for minor price changes, trading opportunities abound.

Scalping has a range of disadvantages, including:

It will require a lot of time and exertion.

Exit management must be highly well-organized and disciplined.

Due to a large number of transactions, transaction costs may be high.

Day traders, who keep positions for a few hours to a day, step up from scalpers. A day trader would not keep a place open past the end of the trading day, avoiding exposure to any market-moving news that might emerge overnight.

Day Trading Vs. Swing Trading

When you day trade, you open and close trades on the same day. The phenomenon of help and resistance is the most critical factor during day trading. In day trading, the phenomenon of daily patterns plays a vital role. Day trading is dependent on the ebb and flow of buyers' and sellers' emotions. The relation between bubble emotions (such as greed, fear, etc.) and investor mentality (such as bull, bear, and so on) generates opportunities for capital gain or loss.

Typically, the acceleration of a stock price exhibits patterns of recurrent swings. Occasionally, the phenomenon of swings provides an incentive for capital gain. Swing trading is a stock market investment strategy in which a tradable asset is kept for one to several days to benefit from price shifts or swings. Swing trading has a significantly higher profit potential than day trading. Swing trading necessitates more patience and experience in the stock market. The trade may be held for a few days or weeks by the trader. It all depends on how much the stock prices trend and swing. In general, a swing trader determines a degree of satisfaction concerning swing duration.

However, due to unforeseen trend lengthening or shortening, a swing trader's anxiety level may rise, or his comfort zone may be disturbed; these moments are crucial, and an inexperienced swing investor may make impatient decisions. Swing trading necessitates calm action and in-depth fundamental and technical analysis of a stock, company, market, and economy. With a deeper understanding of upcoming trends and swings, a professional swing trader buys when people are selling and sells when people are buying. He avoids overreacting to news, events, and emotions. He takes pride in riding a pattern until it shows signs of reversal or retracement. "Retracements are temporary price reversals that occur within the context of a larger trend. The significant observation here is that these price reversals are only temporary and do not indicate a shift in the overall trend. A trend that does not retrace is unhealthy or dangerous. Because a trend is defined as "a series of higher highs and higher lows," the trend must end when the stock fails to establish a higher high and instead sets a lower low. A lower high is undesirable, but it does not signal the end of the trend. After making a lower high, the stock could retrace, never making a lower low, and then push above the previous high to make a higher high. The establishment of the lower low is the final nail in the coffin of a bullish trend. Normally, the trend is over once the lower low is reached. It is known as a **Reversal**." An investor's objective is to make small profits on - day. The swing trader's risk tolerance is high because they have relatively broad profit goals. What comes to fruition in achieving goals is focused on better understanding the behavior patterns and investor tendencies. The impatient person gets dollars, while the patient and wise investor profits. It appears that there is a straightforward trade setup when the first day of the trade, but swing setups remain unclear. Day trading sacrifices the ability to trade profit on a little. Swing trading is a hybrid of day and long-term trading, with transactions lasting anywhere from a few days to several weeks. Swing traders are searching for multi-day chart trends that will allow them to profit from more significant price fluctuations than they would usually see in a single day. Swing trading is, at the very least, superior to day trading in this regard. This style appeals to many people because it provides an acceptable balance between trades' pace and time commitments.

Who Is a Swing Trader?

We have a clearer understanding of trading styles now, and so we identify swing traders as traders with a multi-day to multi-week period. they use a mix of fundamental and technical research to help with their investment decisions

If the market is range-bound or on average, the trend will last a long time is inconsequential: A swing trader won't hold onto a spot for long enough to be crucial more competitive the market, the more short-term swings.

Advantages of Swing Trading

Swing trading has many advantages, particularly for those who are new to trading:

✚ Time

trades that last for a brief period need constant observation. In contrast, the majority of long-term transactions may not be sufficient and have an excessive degree of trading discipline

Since swing trading is more beginner-friendly, it uses a different time frame. This type of trader makes fewer analyses and trades over more extended periods. It means they spend more time thinking about their decisions, but they need to put a small number of trades.

Benefiting From Longer Trends

Although scalping and swing trading both look for short-term volatility, users will profit from the longer-term trends. Analysis performed on larger timeframes is often stays reliable over more extended periods, while analysis performed on smaller timeframes is susceptible to noise and questionable market fluctuations. It has the added effect of causing each trade to be more profitable since other trades are involved in the process.

Cost Efficiency

Spread is one of the keys to trading, the gap between the bid and ask rates. Spreads can be minimal in time, but they are often incurred when you sell, thereby eating into your income from selling frequently.

The spread is less of their trades matters for swing traders because they make less of them and hold them for a longer time. The spread usually tends to be smaller, less volatile and tends to have smaller profit numbers.

A Larger Range of Indicators

The four-hourly, regular, and weekly swing trading time units allow you to get the most out of the simplest indicators.

A regular candlestick closing above the 20-period moving average, On a 5-minute chart, for example, is far more reflective than the same candlestick closing above the moving average. Longer time frames generally yield more reliable results, and the best swing trading strategy will benefit from this.

Exploiting Larger Price Movements

Traders who engage in swing trading can profit from large price fluctuations or oscillations that are hard to obtain on a single day. The higher the market uncertainty, the more trading opportunities it provides. Traders who engage in swing trading can profit from large price fluctuations or oscillations that are hard to obtain on a single day. The higher the market uncertainty, the more trading opportunities it provides.

Associated Risks

- **Swap fees accumulate:** Swap fees are regular interest rate fees that are paid on overnight positions. While these fees aren't a problem for scalpers or day traders, they can add up quickly when trading for more extended periods.

- **Fundamental risk:** Outside of trading hours, economic and political trends can impact the financial markets, disrupting a trend and impacting your trading strategy.

The Best Instruments for Swing Trading

Swing trading strategies can be used on several instruments, from ETFs, Options, and all CFD instruments, such as stocks, Forex, commodities, and even indices.

Swing trading in the Forex market enables traders to quickly take advantage of good liquidity and enough flexibility to produce interesting price changes.

The following are examples of the common currencies for swing trading in Forex:

- **Euro:** AUD/EUR, EUR/CAD, EUR/JPY, and EUR/GBP are some of the currency pairs.

- **Japanese Yen:** USD/JPY, JPY/CAD, and JPY/GBP are some of the currency pairs.

- **British Pound:** GBP/AUD, GBP/CAD, and GBP/CHF pairs.

- **U.S. Dollar:** NZD/USD, USD/CAD, AUD/USD, and EUR/USD pairs.

Indices are also very appealing tools for the best stock swing trading strategy:

- The DAX30 CFD

- The CAC40 CFD

- The Dow Jones 30 CFD

- The Nasdaq 100 CFD

- The Nikkei 225 CFD

Stocks have higher bid/ask spreads than currencies, making them weak candidates for swing trading, but you have to pay the spread once. The same applies to 'in the case of any other exotic currency pairs, such as the USD.

Which Time Frame is best?

This is a free-form answer, open-ended question. The analysis of these patterns and how long they can last depends on you.

How to Start Trading

Do you want to start swing trading right away? <u>You can begin by following the simple steps below:</u>

- **Create an account**

- **Get your trading platform and install it:** MetaTrader 4 or MetaTrader 5 are the two options.

- **Log in to the site and trade for the first time:** Now, all you have to do is pick an asset and position your first trade.

The next move is to build a plan once you have your account and platform set up and understand how to trade. In the sections below, I've listed some of my favorite swing trading strategies. A swing trader likes to collect dividends, so he acts early during a company's book closing days.

Swing trading is a word that you might have heard among traders, but do you know what it means? In this post, we'll go through the basics of swing trading, including what it is and how to use it, as well as the best swing trading indicators, swing trading strategies, and more.

CHAPTER 2
Swing Trading Strategy

Swing trading is a method of trading rather than a strategy. The time horizon defines this style, and numerous techniques can be used. As a result, determining the best forex swing trading strategy can be difficult.

These strategies are not limited to swing trading or even Forex, and they are based on the principles of help and resistance, as with most technical approaches. These ideas offer you two options for trading strategies: tracking the trend or trading against it. It's helpful to visually recognize price action, or the movement of an asset's price on a map, for any kind.

I'll present you with a list of the most common swing trading strategies, along with a summary of their usefulness.

Trend Trading

Trading with the latest fads is an excellent way to get started in forex trading. Trading techniques have a trend. Therefore, it is the best swing trading strategy; for this reason, it can also be considered an ideal trading strategy.

If we look for patterns in markets, we can also recognize that they do not always travel straight. And when they are eventually winning or losing, they swing in linear movements. To detect an increase in the market, search for higher peaks and lower lows, as long as an advance in the other direction around lower highs. Catching a short trend is the perfect way to go about swing trading.

Counter-Trend Trading

The following approach is the polar opposite of the first. We use the same concepts to detect relatively short-term patterns, but this time we're trying to benefit from how often these trends break down.

Keep in mind what I said earlier:

Higher highs and higher lows indicate an uptrend.

Lower highs and lower lows indicate a downtrend.

You'll notice how a pattern can be accompanied by a cycle of retracement before the trend resumes. During this time of reversion, a counter-trend trader will try to capture the swing. To do so, we'd look for a break in the pattern. Uptrend will be when a new high is met with successive failures. If prices are declining, what we have is a rising trend. When they are going in the opposite direction of the opposite direction is an accurate market correction.

It is vital to retain firm discipline while counter-trending if the price shifts against you. If the market continues its downward trend, you must be able to admit you were wrong and close the trade.

If you want to experiment with trading the currencies in the marketplace, the Forex is an excellent place to start. What is the reason for this? It's simple: the market is open 24 hours a day, five days a week, so you can trade whenever it's convenient for you. It's also a very volatile market, which means there's plenty of space for the best swing trading strategy to succeed.

Moving Average Strategy

Since swing trading is a style, deciding the best moving average strategy for swing trading is difficult. However, using moving averages, I will suggest some of the best times for swing trading.

Swing traders, on the other hand, typically take a different approach. They often trade on wider timeframes (4H, Daily) and retain their positions for more extended periods. As a consequence, a regular chart could be the best MT4 swing trading strategy. In any case, swing traders should select an SMA first and then use longer-period moving averages to avoid early signals and noise. Four moving averages that can be particularly useful for swing traders are mentioned below:

1. **20/21 period:** When it comes to short-term swing trades, some traders tend to use the 21 moving average. Amid a trend, the price tends to respect it and also signals shifts in the trend.

2. **50 periods:** Traders commonly use the 50-period moving average as a

regular moving average for swing trading. Many traders use this as a balance between being short or long.

3. **100 periods:** Round numbers have their allure; numbers like 100 are no exception. It is especially effective for resistance and support on a regular or weekly basis.

4. **200/250 period:** The 200 moving average has the same characteristics as the 250 moving average. Since it depicts a year of price action, the 250 cycle moving average is a common alternative for daily charts (a year contains about 250 trading days)

✚ Bollinger Band Strategy

The Bollinger band is a well-known swing trading measure that can help traders identify possible market reversal points. I'll now teach you how to use the Bollinger Band indicator to build the best swing trading strategy. The Bollinger Band is composed of three curves that are generated using standard deviations and a moving average. The lower and upper bands are standard deviations of the middle band, based on a moving average set for a specific time. The central line is typically the 20-day moving average, with the lower and upper bands separated by two standard deviations. If the underlying quote crosses outside of the upper Bollinger band, it is considered "overbought," implying that it is time to take profits and liquidate.

On the other hand, the underlying is called "oversold" when it falls below the bottom Bollinger band. It indicates that prices will be able to offset losses. As the underlying quote rises from the bottom bar, the middle band serves as the first line of resistance, as continued exchange beyond the central line typically leads to the upper line. If a quote falls below the upper line, the middle line becomes the first level of support; if it fails to stay at the middle band, the lower band becomes the next level to watch.

Improving Your Strategies

A wider variety of products is better if you're interested in swing trading. The first is to try to time the trade to coincide with a long-term pattern. While we looked at an hourly chart in the examples above, it may help look at a longer-term chart to get a sense of the long-term trend. Attempt to trade only when your course coincides with the long-term trend.

Using a secondary technical predictor to validate your thinking is another way to boost your swing trading strategy. If you're a counter-trend trader considering selling, check the RSI (Relative Strength Index) to see if it means the market is overbought.

A Moving Average (M.A.) is another valuable indicator for swing trading. A moving average (M.A.) smooths out prices to provide a clearer image of the trend. Since an M.A. includes older price details, it's a simple way to see how current prices relate to previous ones.

Managing Risk in Forex

You may have learned that the vast majority of traders lose money while trading Forex. It is important to remember, however, that this is also true for effective traders. The reality is that no trader ever wins 100 percent of the time; you may misjudge the market, it may change suddenly, or you may make a mistake. Risk management and money management are crucial in this case.

Before you can learn how to win in trading, mainly Forex, you must first learn how to lose. It's all right to incur minor losses to gain large quantities. In this market, if you can tolerate early failures, you have the potential to guarantee that your income will outweigh your losses. <u>Swing trading risk management tips include:</u>

- **Assess your overall permissible loss.** Although you certainly want to make money on your next trade, it's also essential to think about how much you're willing to gamble. If you understand this formula, you can set a stop loss to close your position if it goes in the wrong direction.

- **Don't place all of your money on a single trade.** Your whole trading portfolio should never be risked on a single transaction. You risk losing something if you do so. A widely accepted rule is that you should never lose more than 2% of your account equity on any single transaction.

- **To diversify your risk, consider increasing your account balance.** While an account can be opened with as little as €200, it is recommended that you start with a more considerable amount. It means you'll have enough money in your account to trade a wide range of assets and spread your risk. Since swing trading is a longer-term strategy than day trading or scalping, you'll need more margin on your positions to manage market volatility.

- **Understand your risk profile.** One of the first things you can do before you begin trading is assess your risk and volatility tolerance. To put it another way, when will we become worried about the loss? Assume you have a €20,000 savings account balance and lose €2,000, or 10% of your savings. Would your world come crashing down, or would you consider it a minor setback? The way you handle this setback will have an impact on the level of risk you're willing to take in trading.

Swing trading is a short and long-term trading technique, as you now know. Money management swing trading is a trading technique that is heavily reliant on risk and capital management.

The Best Swing Trading Tools and Indicators

You can use a range of methods and metrics to increase the chances of success by using swing trading strategies.

<u>Here is a couple that I hope you'll enjoy:</u>

- **Correlation Matrix:** One element of analysis that allows the wise trader to behave with trust is the connection between Forex pairs, commodities, or stock indices.

- **Mini Charts:** You can use a mini charting tool to look at different time units on a single graph. It eliminates the trader's need to turn from the swing trading chart W1 to the D1 chart to find his entry point on the H4 chart.

- **Mini Terminal:** In a matter of seconds, you can open a spot in MetaTrader, as well as trades with fixed euros or percentage risk, using the mini terminal app. In reality, this Expert Advisors gives you a variety of details about the stock market or the currency pair you're trading, such as the latest trend, current momentum, and the intensity of contemporary movements.

Tips for Forex Swing Trading

Now that you've learned the fundamentals of swing trading and some effective Forex swing trading strategies, here are some of my best swing trading tips:

Trade in line with the long-term trend. While you might be looking at a shorter-term time chart (e.g., H1 or H4), a longer-term chart (D1 or W1) may also help determine the long-term trend. After that, make sure you're not betting against a broader pattern. Swing trading is much better when you trade with the movement rather than against it.

Use Moving Averages to your advantage (M.A.s). By smoothing shorter-term market swings, the M.A. indicator will assist swing trading by detecting patterns. Since the M.A. contains previous prices, it is a quick way to see how the current price compares to previous prices.

Make use of any leverage. Leverage allows you to take on a greater role than your deposit allows typically, allowing you to increase your earnings (and losses). Leverage, when used wisely, will help you make the most of profitable trades.

Exchange a diverse selection of currency pairs. To find the best options, keep an eye on as many currency pairs as possible. The Forex market will always provide you with trading opportunities; you have to find the ones that best fit your trading style, strategies, and risk tolerance. Trading several pairs will help you diversify your portfolio and stop placing all your eggs in one basket.

Keep an eye out for swaps. Swaps are a form of trading fee that is applied to overnight positions. To better manage your capital, you must consider the cost of these swaps.

Achieve a profit/loss ratio that is optimistic. Swing trading, whether on H4 or a regular basis, allows you to benefit from significant market swings, enabling you to achieve higher profit ratios than scalping.

Set your feelings aside. Swing trades should be executed as part of a well-established Forex trading plan and strategy rather than traded on emotion.

Choosing a Broker

You must first select a broker before you can begin trading. A Forex broker will provide you with access to the markets you wish to trade as well as a trading platform on which to execute your transactions. <u>Some brokers, however, are stronger than others, so keep the following in mind when making your decision:</u>

- Is there a local regulator in your region that controls them?

- **Low transaction costs.** Trading expenses include spreads, swaps, and exchange commissions, all of which can eat into your earnings. As a result, it's crucial to think about **expected trading costs.**

- **Trade sizes are adaptable.** A regular Forex lot, or trading deal, is equal to 100,000 of the pair's base currency, or the first currency mentioned (for example, one lot of EUR/USD is similar to EUR 100,000). If you're a new trader, this could be too much, so see if your broker offers mini (0.1) and micro (0.01) lots for trading.

- **Price data that is updated in real-time.** You'll need the most up-to-date market data to make informed trading decisions. In their trading platforms, good Forex and CFD brokers can provide live price info.

- **Available leverage.** What kind of leverage does the broker provide? In Europe, controlled brokers can provide Professional Clients with leverage of up to 1:500 and Retail Clients with leverage of up to 1:30.

- **There is a minimum deposit number.** What is the smallest sum needed to begin trading? You can finance your trading account with as little as €200 at Admirals. It helps you start small without taking a large risk and progressively increasing as you gain market behavior and independent trading psychology experience.

- **Tools for risk management.** With volatility security and negative balance protection, Admirals will help you reduce your trading risk.

- **Trading versatile styles.** Will the broker encourage you to day trade and scalp besides swing trading if that's part of your strategy?

- **Investing in education**. Is there a collection of tools and services available from the broker to help you succeed as a trader?

Volatile trading is excellent for swing trading as it offers many opportunities. Swing trading takes a considerable amount of time to track the market, but the criteria are not as demanding as trading types with shorter time frames. Swing trading strategies, even if you prefer intraday or scalping, will provide you with some diversification in your performance as well as the opportunity for additional gains.

Swing trading is not for all, so it's best to practice risk-free on a demo trading account first. Sign up for an Admiral's trial account and begin risk-free testing of your swing trading strategies on the markets.

CHAPTER 3
Why 95% Of Traders Lose Money(Forex Trading)

A well-known fact is that a large percentage of forex traders lose money. According to various websites and blogs, 70%, 80%, and even more than 90% of forex traders lose money and leave. Those are discouraging figures for anyone seeking to make a living in the forex market. Although the figures differ depending on the study, the fact remains that the majority of traders lose money when they sell. 10-20% of all F.X. traders make a profit, according to brokerreviews.org. Many forex traders do better than that, according to the forex website DailyFX, but new traders still struggle to gain traction in this market. <u>The list below will show you some of the most</u> <u>common reasons why forex traders lose money and help you become part of</u> <u>the elusive 5% of active traders:</u>

Inadequate financial management

Inadequate planning

Inadequate policy

Inadequate risk control

Lack of a trading plan

Inadequate strategy or strategies for performance

Psychological and emotional fatigue

All of the above factors influence trading results, but there are more complex reasons why most forex traders lose money.

The majority of people who struggle in forex trading do so because they lack a rational understanding of trading and trading. The idea of becoming wealthy overnight motivates many people to enter the forex market. They are enticed by the luxury of wealthy traders' lifestyles. They don't consider the challenges they've faced along the way or the years of experience they've gained to get to that point.

The majority of people are only interested in receiving immediate gratification, which is reflected in their trading approach in the stock market. It is the incorrect way to trade Forex. In trading, you don't become good overnight.

Why Forex Traders Fail

Most people do not consider trading success criteria and intend to succeed with only essential talent and skills. You must have a rational outlook and a strong understanding of your abilities to succeed in forex trading. Traders spend hours in front of computer screens, gazing at price charts, waiting for trading opportunities to present themselves.

You will need both patience and diligence to take advantage of opportunities. To be successful in forex trading, you must possess a variety of skills. You will fail to succeed if you do not have a trading plan or strategy in place.

Trading on the forex market is often mentally exhausting, and many traders cannot study the market. They become bored, irritated, or exhausted, and they begin to make rash trades without considering any relevant factors. To amuse you, I'll say that the 95 percent failure rate is a little high, but it's fair to say that forex trading isn't easy by any stretch of the imagination. Both traders who are struggling to make progress and are losing trades have the same traits. <u>These are the following</u>:

Having unreasonable assumptions about the market

Overcomplicating their research

 Investing with money, they can't afford to lose (money for bills, mortgage, etc.)

Using a lousy money management approach

Chasing market noise and price instead of using accurate data

Wasting too much time over charts instead of trading

To find out how many points you have, go through the list of characteristics listed above. Have you made the same mistakes? If you have trouble trading forex, you may be. However, don't worry; you're not the only one who makes these mistakes. All traders face these issues, and these issues prevent them from being active in forex trading.

Why Does the Forex Market Still Make You Doubtful?

We must understand more about why Forex traders struggle before we move on to the technical aspects. The Forex market defies anything we have traditionally believed to be authentic.

This scenario, combined with the market's tendency to take one step forward and two steps back, produces circumstances that we are unsure how to handle.

Remember this: once you grasp this concept, you will correct the other processes and be on the right track.

I'll explain. There's still a sense of losing out on the market, whether you've made money or lost money. If you made a profit, you'd wonder why you sold so soon, and if you lost, you'd wonder why you didn't hesitate because you might have made a profit. To put it another way, you will never be happy.

The market's ability to go in all directions produces a paradox that exhausts us. You will still have concerns in the business. The market tests us and takes us on an emotional journey; once a transaction is completed, a new one starts. The emotional journey begins again; the rollercoaster continues to drop more and more people.

I've seen traders who make enormous profits for months and then lose it on one poor day. But it doesn't end there; there are technical standards for success in the Forex industry, which run counter to our intuition and what we've experienced during our lives.

For example, in sports, if the opposing team scores, we strive to play harder so that it does not happen again; however, in forex trading, you must be patient, do not play harder, and even give up the trading day entirely.

Another example: In business, you'll do all you can to save the company; in trading, you'll learn to cut your losses early, using stop loss, and you shouldn't wait for the price to come back, or you'll lose even more.

To summarize, most traders struggle, and it isn't always their fault; but, if you can understand why and change your attitude, it would be a small step forward for you and a significant step forward for your career.

Reasons Why 95% of Forex Traders Struggle.

Lack of a trading plan

The most obvious explanation why nearly 95 percent of traders struggle in forex trading is a lack of a proper trading strategy. The only way to become a consistent and profitable trader is to approach trading as an honest company. A trading strategy is a systematic approach to assessing and screening currency pairs to evaluate the risk you should take or open to you. It will allow you to set long-term and short-term investment goals.

Any good trading strategy would provide knowledge about the trading system you would employ. However, as inexperienced traders begin to invest in the market, it can be difficult for them to develop a trading strategy. There is an easy solution to this issue, and answering a few basic questions will help you develop an effective exchanging technique. <u>These are the questions:</u>

What time of day do you want to trade?

How long do you plan to hold your positions/trades?

How much are you able to put on the line?

What are your trading objectives?

Which currency pairs are you interested in?

If you combine an effective trading plan with an efficient established strategy, you will increase your chances of making profitable trades in the forex market. The plan will be discussed next.

Lack of strategy or tactics that lead to success

The absence of a successful trading strategy significantly decreases traders' chances of success in the forex market. So, what is the most effective method for determining whether or not a plan is profitable? You reverse the procedure. Don't be concerned if you're unfamiliar with the term "back-testing." It's straightforward.

Back-testing a strategy is as easy as taking the strategy and applying it in the charts using data from previous years. For example, if your approach is based on a harmonic pattern, you must look into the market action of 2018 to see how many traders used that particular harmonic pattern that year. You should not restrict the testing of a system to one year or 100 traders.

After you've completed the exam, you'll know whether or not a plan was profitable. The outcome of the test will decide this. So, if you discover that 60 of 100 trades were losers and 40 were winners, does that suggest that this technique isn't worth it? No, it means that a trader would win four trades and lose six trades on average if they use this strategy. However, if the trader employs genuine risk management tactics, they will succeed in the forex market.

Poor risk management

Bad money management is one of the most common mistakes traders make in forex trading. Risk management is essential when investing in any market.

The same is true for the forex market. Traders should choose lot sizes depending on the amount of money in their accounts. It is what distinguishes good traders from those who struggle in forex trading. Good traders stop losing money by successfully handling their assets.

Any trader with weak risk management is unlikely to win many trades, which is one of the key reasons they fail in forex trading.

Trading is psychologically Exhausting.

Many of the issues that occur in forex trading are psychological. Traders who give up too quickly will not succeed in forex trading because they lack the required psychological traits and character. The top 5% of traders devote a significant amount of time to personal trends and fine-tuning their trading strategies, which is essential for a promising trading career.

Befriending the Market

The business isn't something you beat; it's something you learn about and jump into when a pattern emerges. Simultaneously, if you try to get too much from the market with too little money, the market will shake you out. Traders who have the mentality of "beating the market" are more likely to trade too aggressively or against trends, a recipe for disaster.

Low Start-Up Capital

The majority of currency traders begin by looking for a way to get out of debt or make fast cash. To produce significant returns on a limited amount of initial money, forex marketers often urge you to exchange large lot sizes and use high leverage.

It would help if you had equity to make money, and you can make excellent returns on limited capital in the short term. However, with a limited amount of capital and a high level of risk due to excessive leverage, you'll find yourself being emotionally involved in each swing of the market's ups and downs, as well as jumping in and out at the worst possible moments.

You can prevent this problem by never trading with too little money. For someone who wants to start trading on a shoestring, this constraint is challenging to overcome. If you're new to trading, $1,000 is a decent place to start (micro lots or smaller). Failure is certain if you do.

Giving in to Greed

Some traders assume that they must suck every last penny out of a price change. Every day, money can be made in the forex markets. They are trying to get the last pip before a currency pair turns can lead to you holding positions for too long, putting you at risk of losing a lucrative trade. The answer seems to be self-evident: don't be selfish. It's good to aim for a decent profit, but there are plenty of pips available. Since currencies change daily, there's no need to get the last pip; the next chance is just around the corner.

Indecisive Trading

Trading guilt is something that can happen to someone at any moment. It happens when a trade you open doesn't work, and you begin to think you made a wrong choice. When you've finished trading, the market reverts to its normal position.

In this scenario, you must choose a course and stick to it. All of your flipping back and forth would result in you losing small amounts of money at a time before your investment capital is exhausted.

Trying to Pick Tops or Bottoms

Many new traders attempt to predict currency pair turning points. They'll enter a trade on a pair, and as it proceeds to go in the wrong direction, they'll add to their position, optimistic that it'll turn around this time. If you trade in this manner, you will end up with much more exposure than you expected, as well as a highly negative trade.

It's better to trade in the direction of the trend. The fact that you correctly selected one bottom out of ten attempts isn't worth the bragging rights. Wait for confirmation on the trend shift if you believe the trend is about to change and want to trade in the new potential direction.

Pick up the bottom of an uptrend, not a downtrend, if you want to pick up a spot at the bottom. Choose a top while the market makes a corrective step higher, rather than an uptrend that is part of a broader downtrend if you want to open a spot at the top.

Refusing to Be Wrong

Some trades aren't meant to be. It's human nature to try to be perfect, but you can't always be. Instead of sticking to the illusion of being right and ending up with a zero-balance trading account, traders should admit that they are often wrong and move on.

It's difficult to admit that you've made a mistake, but sometimes you have to. Either you went into the company for the wrong reasons, or things didn't go as expected. In this case, it is best is to admit and abandon the exchange and move on to the next investment.

Buying a System

On the internet, there are numerous so-called forex trading systems for sale.

Some traders are on the lookout for the elusive 100% accurate forex trading method. They continue to buy and test systems before giving up, concluding that there is no way to win.

You must agree that there is no such thing as a free lunch as a new trader. Winning at forex trading, like everything else, necessitates hard work. Instead of buying useless systems from shady marketers on the internet, you will achieve success by developing your tool, plan, and system.

Takeaway

You would be psychologically torn apart by the forex market. The financial sector is a highly competitive and brutal arena that has made grown men weep. Since there will be many ups and downs in the forex market, you must understand your limitations and strive to strengthen them. While the majority of forex traders lose money, this does not guarantee that you will lose money as well. Improve your risk management, build a strong trading plan with a good trading strategy, and improve your weaknesses. Only then would you be able to succeed as a forex trader.

CHAPTER 4
How To Be Among The 5% Who Succeed In Trading

Speaking with an old friend about money and wealth and why some people have it, others (the majority) do not. "What do you think is the key reason that such a small number of people become rich in this world?" my friend inquired. Although that is a loaded question that could take some time to respond to, the main answer is that most people are just not psychologically prepared to do what it takes to become wealthy regularly. In trade, it operates the same way. Most traders lose income, just as most people remain in the middle to lower classes economically. For the most part, the causes are very, very similar. When you strip out the factors that aren't fair, such as being born in a poor part of the world or having a serious physical or mental handicap, the primary reasons why 95 percent of people struggle at things like trading, company, and wealth trend are pretty much the same.

Things the best 5% of traders in the world do differently

Stay in Trades Longer

I guarantee you that the top 5% of traders stay in trades even longer than you are. In the markets, use time to your advantage. Don't be tempted to close trades too soon. Allowing them to ride increases the chances of catching a big market change that will earn you some significant profits; this is how the top 5% of traders got to where they are.

Place your stops correctly and intelligently (not greedily). Properly positioning your stop losses is one of the most important factors that can make or break you as a trader. Without a doubt, the top 5% of traders have mastered the art and ability of stop loss placement, and you will need to as well. The most useful advice I can give you on this subject is to use a larger stop loss than you think you should. Most of the time, traders have a clear understanding of market direction or want a good entry signal, but their stop is too close and is hit simply by the normal regular price fluctuations. The important thing is to position your stop outside these normal price ranges and above nearby main levels.

Trade with clean charts and pay attention to the end-of-day data.

Traders who consistently make money over a long period (not just a few fortunate months) understand the importance of focusing on clean end-of-day charts to get the most accurate picture of the market. They concentrate on higher time frame charts, specifically the regular time frame, and make their trading decisions based on price action data from that time frame. You'll be hard-pressed to find some long-term profitable traders who focus exclusively on short time frames and scalping. Scalping or short-term trading is a useless endeavor that increases the operational difficulty, adds hours to the market exposure, and lowers the odds of success in the long term.

Utilize a Clear Arsenal of Trading Strategies

Professional traders are well-versed in the markets and precisely know what they're looking for. They have a set of setups and trading strategies in mind, and they patiently wait for everything to fall into place for their entry signal to appear. To succeed, you need a CLEAR arsenal of trading strategies; you can't just "wing it" and hope to "figure it out." All you'll "find out" is that you were mistaken and that you wasted money.

Make a trading strategy that involves printing out the best setups you're looking for in trading. If you're trading price action, for example, you'd have a printout of the pin bar signal and its variants, as well as other price action signals. You ought to have a plan that you go to each time to examine the charts and take exchange.

Apply Sound Risk / Reward Per Trade

The top 5% of traders have gotten to where they are because they understand risk and reward. They are good at the science of risk versus return and know how to use it to position stops and targets.

Part of risk/reward understands the risk/reward, which you can do by letting trades run their course without your constant intervention (like the bottom 95 percent do). You will be able to position and exit trades more often as you practice, and your trading performance will increase.

Look for a point of confluence

When you have several confluence variables in a deal, it gives it more "weight" or "authority," which means it has a marginally better chance of working out in your favor. Technical traders understand the value of distorted odds. One way they do so is by deciding what pieces of "proof" on the charts represent "confluence" and waiting for those individual components to come together to form a probable conclusion. You're looking for as much technical chart proof as possible to support your trade.

Thinking and Acting Properly in The Market

The two overarching factors that decide whether or not you can make money, in the long run, are how you think and behave in the market.

You can't get too worked up about your trades, and you can't let the outcomes of your most recent trades affect you too much (recency bias). Trusting yourself and staying cool, calm, and secure in the face of the relentless temptation and adversity of trading is an important part of thinking and behaving properly in the market. The top 5% of traders have spent so much time thinking and acting correctly in the markets that they have built a sort of "sixth sense" in terms of trading instincts and "gut feel" in the market; this is the product of years of thinking and acting correctly in the markets.

Write a Daily / Weekly Market Summary or Journal of Their Trades

To become one of the top 5% of traders, you must become "in tune" with the markets, which means you must learn to recognize what has happened, what is happening, and what could happen next. It is what I mean when I say "reading the market like a novel." When you start writing a regular review of your favorite maps, the charts will begin to make a lot more sense to you, and you'll be following the money trail. Starting this regular market journaling/analysis will elevate your trading to a whole new level.

Treat Trading Like A Business

Professional traders approach trading as if it were a bank. It has losses, computer equipment, internet data, and so on, as well as revenues (winning trades). You make PROFIT when your income exceeds your expenses, just like any other company. Unfortunately, 95% of traders' expenses skyrocket due to losing money by risking too much, trading too much, and not understanding what they're doing.

You must begin to treat your trading as a company by following all of the steps outlined in this lesson and behaving "as if" you are already a highly successful trader. Remember, even though you aren't a hedge fund trader, trade like one.

Get knocked down and immediately get back up (confidence and resilience)

If you want to be a good businessperson, I recommend that you watch the Rocky movies. He was pounded into a bloody pulp and then kept getting up to face more powerful adversaries and returning to the battle, just as you would have to do in the markets.

You'll suffer losses. You may have thought they would run away with the prize, but it was disappointing that you didn't let them win. You may have trades that barely graze your goal and turn and miss, but that should pull you in. You may have many "near misses and losses" as a shape trader, but you are lost if you respond to them. You should be able to get back on your feet and saddle the horse. It's okay if you aren't able to do it. Take some time off from the map before you're calmer. When you fall, you must get back up, unwounded and stronger than before you get angry or distraught.

Takeaway

above all else, maybe above all else, the top 5% of traders know that it is important to understand oneself. Ironically, no one can control the market; all you have to do is master yourself, and your trading will grow as a result.

What do you do to learn to "master" yourself? You must understand that you're not perfect; like anyone else, you're still making business mistakes. Unfortunately, by taking courses to inform yourself better, be less likely to consider failure as a choice, and focused on trading, you will move up from the bottom 95% of traders to the elite 5% of the population. There is no "Holy Grail" to success; it's about learning, knowing where you're going, and doing whatever is required to get there.

CHAPTER 5
The Basics Of Investing And The Stock Market

What is investing?

You can invest in various ways. For others, investing can mean making money; for others, making investments to obtain value, such as self-improvements, such as dedicating time or energy.

In this context, we shall refer to investing as placing money into financial products, investment properties, or into a commercial venture with the intention of profiting.

Investing involves committing resources or funds to various assets to produce a benefit or profit from these investments in the future.

Savings vs. Investing

One issue with investment is that it's also mixed up with speculation (penny stocks or options trading). Investment differs from savings in that it is a more aggressive way of deploying your money. In contrast, saving is commonly interpreted as holding a portion of your income without considering where you are moving your surplus funds.

Investing vs. Speculating

Investing differs from speculation in that speculation is commonly described as looking for high returns on your investments in a short time. Speculation is very high-risk speculation within a very short time frame In the majority of cases. The returns should be consistent with the risks.

Investing in the right tools would help you excel in both creating wealth and outperforming an index. When it comes to investing, my investment tool of choice is Stock Rover. It empowers me to design the most comprehensive dividend-generating screens. Stock Rover is a strong beer. It is just like getting a supercar in your possession to learn how to use the tools properly.

Why should I invest my money?

Investing is important for making your money work for you. Money should work hard for you. Your money is completely secure in the bank. If you put your money where your mouth is, the risk is yours.

Investment is how you manage your financial stability. You will build your wealth while earning an income stream when you need it.

Trend and income are typically generated by various investment vehicles, such as stocks, bonds, or real estate. Investing or doing things the right way will mean a longer working life. When investing seriously, returns will help you to have financial stability in the future.

Here are few compelling reasons to consider investing your money:

Higher Investment Returns

Investing money in an asset is a tradeoff since the investor foregoes the utility of using the money now for his investment in return for a higher utility later.

- Equity investments can produce returns in two ways: dividends and capital gains.

- Investing in a bond may offer incentives to the investor in the form of monthly payouts or coupons offered at predetermined intervals.

- Real estate investing may also provide an owner with rental income and capital gains.

Retirement Plan or FIRE

The vast majority of people invest for their retirement. Since most people rely on their salary income to meet their needs, it is difficult to maintain one's lifestyle after retirement when one does not have a job.

It ensures that everyone must invest a portion of their earnings during their working years to have a nest egg in their retirement years. Previously, the government and businesses offered defined benefit pension programs for employees; however, defined contribution plans are now the standard.

Many young people plan to retire early, so they must invest a greater portion of their income in reaching their goals. The "FIRE" movement has grown in popularity among millennials. Most people nowadays strive for "Financial Independence, Retire Early (FIRE)."

Saving a significant portion of one's income from a young age (as much as 70% of one's income) will enable one to retire at 40-45 rather than 60-65. The FIRE movement promotes a frugal lifestyle both when investing and when retiring early.

- **Tax Efficiency**

Investing will also help you save taxes because there are accounts such as the RRSP, TFSA, 401k, Roth IRA, and others that have reduced to no taxes on your investments.

As governments minimize their burden for financing their citizens' retirement years, these types of accounts have been developed so that citizens can contribute to and finance their retirement.

- **Beat inflation**

Investing is also important for beating inflation. If you do not invest your money and keep it in a checking or savings account, it will lose buying power as inflation eats away at your money's value.

Although reported inflation is currently quite low, real inflation is quite high because education and healthcare costs are rising much faster than reported inflation. Canadian banks do not even pay 2% on savings deposits, which means that your money will depreciate over time if you do not invest.

Even a 2% return may not last long, as other international central banks have cut close to 0% or even lower. It means that when inflation is factored in, you will face a day when your bank deposits receive 0% or even a negative return.

It may be advisable to begin investing in an asset portfolio that exceeds inflation if you want to protect yourself from such a scenario.

- **Achieve Your Financial Goals**

Investing is a very effective method of attaining one's financial objectives. As an individual progresses through life, new financial requirements emerge.

Typically, it begins with the purchase of a home. Even if a home is purchased with a loan, a significant down payment is expected. A person can build up the corpus needed for the down payment by investing in various assets.

Another significant investment target is children's college education. With the skyrocketing tuition these days, parents will begin funding their children's college education as early as possible. Aside from these financial goals, retirement is an ever-present financial target for people in their working lives.

The Risks of Investing

Although there are many benefits to investing, there are also several disadvantages.

- **Losses**

There is no such thing as a truly risk-free investment because there is always the chance of losing your investment. Also, government securities, which are generally recognized as the safest form of investment, are not without risk. Governments may default on their debt, and there have been numerous examples of such defaults throughout history.

- **Needs Investing Knowledge**

Investing necessitates advanced knowledge of finance and various asset classes. Experience is also valuable in investing, as an investor who has seen many economic cycles will generally manage various types of circumstances better than an inexperienced investor.

Since most people lack financial experience, they will need the assistance of a financial advisor. Using the best available financial advisor can be difficult due to possible conflicts of interest. One of the key reasons so many DIY investors avoid mutual funds.

Types of Investment Assets

Investing is inextricably linked to risk, measuring the potential return on investing in a particular asset. In general, the higher the risk of an asset, the higher the investor's anticipated return. For example, as the risk of an investment in stocks is typically higher than a bond, the expected return on stocks is always greater than the expected return on bonds.

There is a diverse range of investment properties, each with a specific risk profile. Some examples of different types of assets are:

stocks

goods and services

fixed income

gold

real estate,

art,

derivatives

Venture capital and private equity capital are examples of alternative investments.

Types of Investing Styles

Aside from the various forms of investment, there are also various types of investing styles, also known as investment strategies. In order of knowledge/effort, the most significant ones are listed below. The investing style approach you choose will be determined by your level of interest in the subject and the amount of time you are prepared to invest.

None of them outperforms the others in terms of yield. Since no man can forecast the future, it is all up to you and Lady Luck.

• Index Investing

This technique is based on John C. Bogle's investing method, in which you will mirror the index rather than beating it and paying high fees.

Index investing is gaining popularity these days. It enables an investor to put their money to work with little awareness and still make a profit. It is also argued that no investor can consistently outperform the index over a long time. Why aim to beat the index if experts are unable to do so is their conclusion.

• Dividend Investing

This strategy focuses on dividend stocks to generate income and use dividend growth to identify high-quality growth stocks. A dividend income stock typically has a higher dividend yield, while a dividend growth stock typically has a lower dividend yield.

To avoid depleting their portfolio, retirees often seek out high-yielding stocks to finance their retirement. This strategy allows you to stop running out of money while still having more leverage over it.

• Value Investing

This method is possibly more analogous to Warren Buffett's investing strategy, in which he seeks out strong companies with an economic moat that are undervalued. Identifying an undervalued stock can be difficult, but when you do, it can be very lucrative.

Valuation is not a straightforward technique, and books have been published about how to do it, as well as hypotheses from academics. This method necessitates patience.

- **Technical Trading**

This tool explores patterns in stock price movement and volume. The trends are often focused on how average investors approach investing, which results in identifiable patterns.

The Risks of Not Investing

So let's get started and take a glance at some of the doom-and-gloom situations you'll have to live with because you won't invest.

Opportunity Loss: The Silent Killer

There is a common and incorrect belief that were investing entails "taking a risk" with your money. Some assume that exposing it to the market means that you will lose it. The way of thinking is backward. In reality, by not showing your money to the market, you will lose money over time–the difference is that the loss will be invisible.

In this scenario, opportunity loss refers to the money you lose out on by not investing. When the profits of savers and investors are compared, it is clear how much money is wasted. Consider the following:

• Saving $200 per month for 25 years at a 0.5 percent annual interest rate from the bank. You will have $63,741.88 at the end of the contract.

• Investing $200 per month for 25 years at a small annual interest rate of 6% (average). You will have $131,674.83 at the end of the contract. Your opportunity costs are the difference between the two figures: $67,932.95. That's right; you did lose the money.

A year you keep your money in savings is a year you miss out on the wonder and glory of compound interest. Why would you do anything like that to yourself?

Inflation: As certain as death and taxes

Inflation is a given, much like death and taxes.

Since all of your money is tucked away in a comfortable, conventional savings account, you can feel secure. You can get to it whenever you want, and you don't have to worry about your savings being wiped out by a market downturn. You'll keep piling new money on top of old, like a dung beetle rolling a tiny ball of garbage up the hill.

You're probably aware that your money would gain very little interest. Most rates are currently about 0.1 percent, which is just a step away from the bank charging you to store your money. "Pish posh," you announce, "I'm all for capital protection." I'll be able to enjoy my fortune in my golden years if I save for years."

But, as you can see, something similar will happen for years to come–inflation. It rises at a steady rate of 2% to 3% every year, far outpacing the paltry 0.1 percent you're getting from the bank. What does this suggest for you? It indicates that your money will lose purchasing power. Can you remember your grandparents saying that "a dollar doesn't go as far as it used to"? That will, unfortunately, be you sooner than you think. Put on your cardigan and sensible shoes, and feed the pigeons in the park right now.

Disaster: It can happen to you

Are you bracing yourself for the worst? And it happens to people regularly. Unexpected job loss or illness will devastate your finances in months, if not weeks. Your accumulated debt will reach a breaking point, rendering your paycheck-to-paycheck life untenable. And, with the extreme weather we're experiencing as a result of global warming, who's to say a hurricane won't rip through your neighborhood, destroying your home? You must be well-prepared.

A well-stocked portfolio is the best financial safety net you can have. Yes, you're putting money into your savings account with the hope of a secure retirement. (Perhaps you'll buy a nice fishing boat and don one of those cool little captain's caps, a little crooked.) But, in the case of a catastrophe, you'd be more than able to put that money into recouping your losses, right? Consider how much more disastrous a catastrophe would be if you didn't have a safety net in place. It is how it will feel:

We all "hope for the best," after all. You are, however, exposing yourself to the whims of the world unless you pair that unbridled optimism with "preparing for the worst." The world, on the other hand, can be a cruel mistress. (Poet Stephen Crane best expressed it.)

I hope these doomsday scenarios have piqued your curiosity. If you don't spend, you're giving up too many chances to make money and develop a prosperous financial future for yourself.

I'm drowning in debt; how do I begin investing?

If you're in debt, paying it off should take precedence overspending. The penalties of being in debt would eat up all of the profits you make from saving. By 5% a year, inflation works against you. So if you raise 10% on your savings, you've won the war. Credit card debt, on the other hand, is even more effective. It works against you at a rate of 40% per year (or 3% per month). It has an eight-fold effect on the economy compared to inflation. As a result, even though you gain 40% on your savings (which is difficult to do regularly), you will end up with nothing. It is why getting out of debt should be your highest priority. The following isn't a how-to guide for getting out of debt, but it does provide some of the most significant and practical steps you can take:

• Keep track of how much you pay against your debt and how much you borrow per month.

• Reduce the amount of money you borrow per month.

• Increase the amount you pay per month against your debt. I'm sure you've heard the advice to stop spending, put your credit cards away, and pay all in cash.

You've certainly heard the advice before, but are you following it? Most likely, not yet. The explanation for this is that breaking old habits is incredibly difficult. If you make too many changes at once, you'll burn out and return to your old habits.

Keeping track of how much you're borrowing and repaying forces you to confront the truth of your debt. It is the most crucial step in resolving the problem. You'll never be able to solve a problem if you don't know how large it is or how good you're solving it. Once you know how much you borrow and how much you pay back per month, you gradually reduce your borrowing amount while gradually increasing your payback amount.

Where should I invest my money?

Aside from the stock market, there are various investment options. Time deposits, shares, mutual funds, foreign currency, precious metals, and several other options are available. For the time being, we'll focus on the most fundamental. Keep in mind that you don't have to choose only one when we go through each one. Effective investors, in practice, invest in a variety of investment vehicles. It's easier to practice them one at a time when you're first starting.

Here are a few examples of where to invest your money:

- **Time Deposits:** A time deposit is a fixed deposit that can't be withdrawn for a given amount of time. The bigger the investment and the longer the period, the greater the returns. Time deposits are useful in the short term. They are, however, almost useless for creating wealth because their returns are often smaller than inflation.

- **Bonds:** A bond is a type of financial instrument that allows an institution to borrow money. When you buy a bond, you're effectively lending the institution money. In exchange, you will be paid interest over the bond's life and the bond's principal sum at the end of the contract.

- **Mutual Funds:** Mutual funds are a means of investing rather than an investment vehicle. Mutual funds are a form of pooled investment vehicle. It applies to the pooling of funds from multiple investors into a single fund. After that, may invest the combined funds in shares, stocks, or even foreign exchange. Mutual funds are often managed by a specialist known as a "fund manager."

- **UITFs (Unit Investment Trust Funds):** A UITF is similar to a mutual fund in that they are both collective investment strategies operated by a fund manager. There are some technological variations, but they aren't important to the current debate.

- **Equities (the Capital Market):** A stock market is where you can invest in publicly traded or publicly traded businesses. When you purchase shares of stock in a corporation, you become a section owner. You will have an interest in the company's ability to expand and profit as a part-owner.

CHAPTER 6
Stock Market

What is the stock market?

The stock market applies to public markets for issuing, purchasing, and selling securities that trade over-the-counter or on a stock exchange. Stocks, also known as equities, reflect fractional ownership in a business, and the stock market is a marketplace for investors to buy and sell such investible assets. A well-functioning stock market is important to economic growth because it allows businesses to access capital from the general public easily.

The Stock Market's Goals – Capital and Investment Income

The stock market plays two critical functions. The first is to provide funding to companies to help them finance and grow their operations. Suppose a corporation issues 1,000,000 shares of stock at $10 each. In that case, it will have $10 million in capital to expand its operations (less whatever expenses the company pays for an investment bank to deal with the stock contribution). The company abstains from bringing about debt and paying revenue charges on that debt by selling stock shares instead of putting away the money needed for growth.

The company abstains from bringing about debt and paying revenue charges on that debt by selling stock shares instead of putting away the money needed for growth.

The stock market's secondary aim is to enable investors – those who buy stocks – to participate in publicly traded companies' income. Stock acquisitions can be beneficial in two ways for buyers. Some stocks pay out dividends daily (a given amount of money per share of stock someone owns). Another way for buyers to benefit from stock purchases is to sell them for a profit if the stock price rises above their purchase price. For example, if an investor purchases shares of a company's stock at $10 per share and the stock's price increases to $15 per share, the investor will sell their shares and benefit 50% on their investment.

The Origins of Stock Trading

While stock trading dates back to the mid-1500s in Antwerp, it is widely acknowledged that modern stock trading began with shares in London's East India Company.

The Beginnings of Investing Trading

Several companies with the name East India were granted charters by the British, French, and Dutch governments in the 1600s. All goods returned from the East were transported by sea, which included difficult journeys often beset by extreme storms and pirates. Shipowners routinely searched out investors to provide funding collateral for a voyage to minimize these risks. Also, investors received a share of the monetary gains if the ship returned successfully, loaded with goods for sale. These are the most punctual instances of limited liability companies (LLCs), and numerous just existed for a solitary voyage.

The East India Company

The East India Company is a British company based in India. There were various reasons that the East India Company was founded. Still, one of them was that it provided a new form of investment that gave investors participation in the whole of a voyage, not just the investment from one voyage as previously. Companies could request higher investments per share thanks to the new business model, allowing them to expand their shipping fleets quickly. Investing in such businesses, which were often shielded from competition by royally-issued charters, became very common because investors could potentially make huge profits.

The First Stock Exchange and the First Shares

Company shares were initially issued on paper, allowing investors to trade them with other investors, but controlled markets did not exist until the London Stock Exchange (LSE) was founded in 1773. Despite a period of considerable financial instability following the LSE's initial establishment, exchange trading managed to survive and flourish in the 1800s.

The New York Stock Exchange's Beginnings

The New York Bourses was founded in 1792 and are the oldest bourses in the world. Though not the first stock exchange in the United States (that honor goes to the Philadelphia Stock Exchange (PSE)), the NYSE grew quickly to become the most important region and eventually the world. The NYSE was situated in a physically strategic location, among some of the country's largest banks and corporations and a major shipping port. The exchange developed share listing requirements and initially charged hefty fees, helping it to become a wealthy institution rapidly.

The Changing Face of Global Exchanges in Modern Stock Trading

For more than two centuries, the NYSE faced little competition domestically, and its expansion was fuelled mainly by an ever-expanding American economy. The London Stock Exchange (LSE) continued to dominate European stock trading, but the New York Stock Exchange (NYSE) attracted an increasing number of large corporations. Many other countries developed their stock exchanges over time, such as France and Germany, but mainly used them as launching pads for businesses that sought to list on the London Stock Exchange or the New York Stock Exchange.

The NASDAQ, which became a favorite home for burgeoning technology firms and gained increased importance during the technology industry boom of the 1980s and 1990s, was one of many exchanges that saw stock trading grow in the late twentieth century. The NASDAQ was the first exchange to operate through a network of machines that performed trades electronically. Trading has become more time and cost-effective as a result of electronic trading. The NYSE faced growing competition from stock exchanges in Australia and Hong Kong, Asia's financial hub, in addition to the growth of the NASDAQ.

The NYSE subsequently merged with Euronext, which took effect in 2000 when the Brussels, Amsterdam, and Paris exchanges joined and Amsterdam in the same undertaking. In 2007, the NYSE/Euronext merger produced the first trans-Atlantic exchange.

Exchanges and Over-the-Counter (OTC) Trading of Stocks

The majority of stocks are exchanged on stock exchanges such as the NYSE or the NASDAQ. Stock exchanges serve as a marketplace for investors to buy and sell stocks. The U.S. government, such as the Securities and Exchange Commission (SEC), keeps the stock market going by protecting investors from unfair practices and maintaining the markets' credibility.

While most stocks are exchanged on exchanges, others are traded over-the-counter (OTC), where buyers and sellers of stocks transact through a broker, or "market maker," specializing in the stock. OTC stocks are those that do not meet the exchange's minimum price or other conditions for listing.

Since OTC stocks are not subject to the same public reporting requirements as stocks listed on exchanges, investors have a tougher time seeking accurate information on the companies that issue them. Since OTC stocks are usually much more thinly traded than exchange-traded stocks, investors must regularly deal with large gaps between the bid and ask OTC stock prices. Exchange-traded funds, on the other hand, are much more liquid, with limited bid-ask spreads.

Investment banks, stockbrokers, and investors are all participants in the stock market.

A large number of people trade stocks daily

When a company first chooses to become a publicly-traded company by selling stock shares, investment banks handle the initial public offering (IPO).

Here's an example of how an initial public offering (IPO) operates. An investment bank is approached by a corporation that wants to go public and sell shares to serve as the "underwriter" of its initial stock offering. After researching the company's overall valuation and deciding what percentage of ownership the company wants to relinquish in the form of stock securities, the investment bank manages the actual issuance of shares in the market for a fee, thus promising the company a fixed minimum price per share. As a result, it is in the investment bank's best interests to ensure that all shares on sale are sold at the highest possible price. Large institutional investors, such as pension funds and mutual fund firms, are the most popular buyers of IPO shares.

The main, or initial, market is where initial public offerings (IPOs) take place. After a stock is released in the main market, all subsequent trade in the stock occurs on stock exchanges, known as the secondary market. The word "secondary market" is a misnomer since this is the market where the vast majority of stock trading occurs daily.

Stockbrokers buy and sell stocks for their customers, who may be institutional investors or individual retail investors. They can or may not even serve as financial advisors.

Stock brokerage firms, mutual fund managers, hedge funds, and investment banks all employ equity research analysts. Some people research publicly traded companies and predict whether their stock will rise or fall in value.

Hedge fund managers, mutual fund managers, and fund investment managers buy and sell massive amounts of stock, particularly hedge funds and exchange-traded funds. When a well-known mutual fund chooses to invest heavily in a particular stock, its price also rises noticeably due to the increased demand.

Indexes of the Stock Market

Different stock market indices' performance is normally tracked and expressed in the stock market's overall performance. Stock indexes are made up of a group of stocks meant to represent the market's aggregate performance. Options and futures contracts, which are also exchanged on regulated markets, are used for trading stock market indexes.

The Dow Jones Industrial Average (DJIA), the Standard & Poor's 500 Index (S&P 500), the Financial Times Stock Exchange 100 Index (FTSE 100), the Nikkei 225 Index, the NASDAQ Composite Index, and the Hang Seng Index are all relevant stock market indexes.

Short Selling, Bull and Bear Markets

The words "bull" and "bear" markets are two of the most fundamental stock market trading principles. The word "bull market" refers to a stock market in which stock prices are continuously increasing. Since most equity investors are buyers rather than short-sellers, this is the type of market in which most investors succeed. When stock values are falling in general, it is called a bear market.

Short selling allows investors to benefit even in bear markets. Short selling is the act of acquiring stock from an exchanging company that holds shares of the stock that the moneylender doesn't claim. After that, the lender sells the borrowed stock securities on the secondary market and collects the proceeds. If the stock price falls as the investor expects, the investor will benefit from buying enough shares to repay the broker for the number of shares they lent at a total price less than what they earned for selling the stock at a higher price earlier.

For example, if an investor assumes that the stock of company "A" will fall from its current price of $20 per share, the investor will make a margin deposit with his broker to borrow 100 shares of the stock. He sells those shares for $20 each, which nets him $2,000 in today's market. If the stock drops to $10 a share, the investor can buy 100 shares for $1,000 and sell them to his broker, leaving him with a $1,000 profit.

Stock Analysis: Market Capitalization, Earnings Per Share, and Financial Ratios

Analysts and investors may consider several factors when forecasting a stock's likely price direction in the future. Here's a rundown of the absolute most broadly utilized stock investigation factors.

The total value of all outstanding shares of a company is its market capitalization or market cap. A business with a higher market capitalization is typically more developed and financially sound.

Exchange regulatory bodies mandate publicly traded firms to provide earnings reports regularly. Market analysts closely monitor these reports, which are published periodically and annually, since they indicate how well a company's business is doing. The company's earnings per share (EPS), which represents the company's profits distributed among all of its outstanding stock shares, is one of the primary factors discussed in earnings reports.

Analysts and investors often review various financial ratios that are meant to show a publicly-traded company's financial stability, profitability, and growth potential. <u>A few main financial ratios that investors and analysts consider are as follows:</u>

- **P/E Ratio:** The ratio of a company's stock price to its earnings per share (EPS). A higher P/E ratio means that investors are willing to pay higher per-share rates for a company's stock because they anticipate its growth and stock price to increase.

- **Debt to Equity Ratio:** This is a key indicator of a company's financial health. It indicates how much of a company's activities are financed by debt and funded by equity investors. It's preferable to have a lower debt-to-equity ratio, which indicates direct support from investors.

- **Return on Equity (ROE) Ratio:** The return on equity (ROE) ratio indicates its net profits about its total equity investment. It is a clear measure of a company's growth potential.

- **Profit Margin:** Investors can consider several profit margin ratios, including operating profit margin and net profit margin. The benefit of looking at the gross margin rather than the actual dollar profit is that it reveals its percentage profitability. For example, a company may make a $2 million profit, but if the profit margin is only 3%, any substantial sales drop may jeopardize its profitability.

Return on assets (ROA), dividend yield, price to book (P/B) ratio, current ratio, and inventory turnover ratio are some other widely used financial ratios.

Value Investing and Growth Investing are the two basic approaches to stock market investing

Analysts and investors use various stock-picking techniques, but almost all are based on two simple stock-buying strategies: **value investing** or **growth investing**.

Value investors usually invest in well-established businesses that have shown consistent performance over time and can pay out regular dividends. While value investors seek to buy stocks when they think the stock price is an undervalued bargain, value investing is more focused on avoiding risk than growth investing.

Growth investors search out businesses with outstanding growth potential in the hopes of maximizing share price appreciation. They are less concerned with dividend income and are more likely to take risks by investing in startups. Growth investors often favor technology stocks due to their high growth potential.

Why should I Invest In Stock?

You'll have enough money saved up at some point to say, "Wow, I should spend this somewhere." If you're brand-new to the stock exchange or intend to refresh your mind, this book is for you.

I've listed 15 compelling reasons why you should invest in stocks below. Finally, I give my two cents on why stock market investing can be so successful.

To begin, let us look at the hard facts about stock investing before moving on to some less discussed (but still important) personal and professional reasons to invest:

- **To Grow Your Money, Invest in Stocks**

It is the most fundamental reason to buy, and it is often at the heart of why people purchase stocks. When done correctly, you can expect your money to rise at a rate of 7% to 10% per year over the long term.

If you put $10,000 in the stock market and it rises at an annual growth rate of 7%, you would have doubled your money by then.

Consider it for a moment. Imagine you put $10,000 into an account ten years ago, invested it in stocks, and made some trades, and now you have your initial $10,000 plus another $10,000 from trading. Consider a longer-term scenario in which you are both a substantial saver and a wise investor. Consider putting $10,000 of your money into the stock market per year for the next 30 years. That's $10,000 this year, $10,000 next year, $10,000 the following year, and so on for the next 30 years.

So, over 30 years, you'll have spent $300,000 in stocks ($10,000 a year x 30 years). Let's say you get the same average annual returns as we did above, which is 7% per year. So you've put $300,000 into your account over 30 years, how much do you have at the end of time?

You know it'll be more than the $300,000 you put in over 30 years because the money will have risen due to your equity investments. But it's the size of the expansion that's shocking. The $10,000 per year investment will now be worth $1,010,730 after 30 years. Over 30 years, $10,000 invested annually will grow to more than a million dollars. Now, $300,000 of the million dollars is your annual investment in the stock market. However, the remaining $710,730 is money you earned by investing in stocks.

The critical thing to note is that investing in the stock market will help you develop your wealth dramatically over time. And it's for this reason that people buy stocks.

- **Invest in stocks since they have historically increased in value**

For the last 100 years, stocks have continued to grow. Yes, there have been some nasty crashes, pullbacks, and poor performance stretches. However, as the US and global economies have risen, stocks have developed a steady upward trend.

The market has generally pushed upwards amid several ups and downs along the way. The profit you would have made would have been substantial if you had kept stocks for 30, 40, or 50 years.

In reality, a single dollar invested in small-company stocks (also known as small-cap stocks) in 1926 would now be worth nearly $40,000 today.

Many people invest in stocks because the chances are in their favor that the price will rise and earn them money over time.

- **Invest in stocks to benefit from the compounding effect.**

Suppose you receive a reasonable return rate over an extended period (but not particularly long) period (30, 40, 50, 60, or more years). In that case, your investment will have more excellent long-term value.

For example, we discussed how saving $10,000 a year for 30 years and receiving a 7% annual return resulted in a windfall of well over a million dollars. But let's take a look at a timeline that's much longer.

Let's pretend you kept the same plan (investing $10,000 a year and receiving 7% annual returns) for 60 years instead of just 30. Your $10,000 monthly investment has now risen to an astonishing $8,104,668. There's a reason it's referred to as "the magic of compound interest."

Your money will grow in genuinely incredible ways over time if you start early, save regularly, and invest wisely. Having real-world, hands-on experience is the best way to think about investing. There is no substitute for purchasing and selling your stocks.

If you're seeking a place to begin, I suggest two tools to all new investors:

1. **The Motley Fool** is an investment advisory firm. Every month, they publish a comprehensive research report as well as their top stock picks. About ten years ago, they suggested mega-winners Disney, Netflix, and Amazon. The Motley Fool taught me how to invest. It's an excellent resource for stock ideas.

2. **TradingView** is a charting software program. It's a must-have when it comes to choosing when to spend. I use it regularly, and I never buy or sell something without first looking at the map (for example, Apple). I've tried every charting tool available, and this is by far the best. Furthermore, their culture is brimming with creative ideas.

Here's what I advise: Use TradingView to study the best time to buy stock picks from The Motley Fool. That way, you can combine fundamental (what to buy) and technical (when to buy) research to find the best stocks to buy right now.

- **Invest in stocks rather than cash because cash loses value over time.**

Inflation is a curious phenomenon that you've probably heard of before. It stated inflation is the gradual yet steady increase in the price of goods over time.

Remember how your grandfather used to be able to go to the movies for a dollar? Today, going to the film costs $10, $15, or even $20. It is primarily due to inflation, which causes the cost of goods and services to increase over time. What this means is that your hard-earned money is falling in value. I understand; it's frightening.

This time it would not be $10,000 to take out if you save 10,000 dollars and put it under your color mattress for the next 30 years. Yeah, it will still cost $10,000 in US dollars. But it won't be worth as much as it was when you first got it.

If today $10,000 can buy you a wonderful trip around the world, then in 30 years, you can only purchase two days in a local hotel if you take it out of your mattress.

I will not discuss too much about inflation because it shifts over time. But keep in mind that when your money is in cash, its value is slowly eroding.

How easily does it deteriorate? That is dependent on the current inflation rate.

It is considering that since the year 2000, the annual inflation rate has been mostly between 1% and 4%. That means your money's purchasing power depreciates by 1% to 4% every year.

If you purchase Treasury bonds or place your money at your local bank on a Deposit Certificate (CD), you will possibly win enough to avoid inflation. Even so, it's not a perfect deal because you might make a lot of money in the stock market.

Also, for example, the United States inflation rate in 2018 was 2.4% every year. The best CD price I could locate online was 2.7 percent each year on a six-year CD from American Financial Institution.

Although this is a substantial change over the current rate of inflation, it is not by much. As a consequence, the value of your money is essentially unchanged.

Think about it like this, if you have saved enough money to buy a new Honda today, and put it;

Under your mattress: you'll be able to buy a bicycle in 30 years.

Invest in a certificate of deposit (CD): you'll be able to buy a nicer Honda in 30 years.

Invested wisely in the stock market: you'll be able to buy a Maserati in 30 years.

- **Invest in stocks because they will yield a higher return than other types of investments.**

When compared to other investment options, stocks have historically produced more wealth for investors. Buying stocks has outperformed buying shares, buying a house, and most other investment options in the United States on average. Investing in residential real estate could be an exception (for example, buying an apartment building and renting out the tenants' units). When you consider both the steadily appreciating value of the property and the value of the rent you collect, research suggests this will return about the same as stocks over time.

In a later post, I'll go through some other comparisons, but for now, keep in mind that stocks have traditionally been one of the best ways to grow your wealth.

- **Invest in stocks because they are simple to manage.**

If you're fortunate sufficient to have some savings, you have several options for where to put your money. You might invest in real estate, shares, start a small company, mutual funds, precious coin collections, and much more.

Stocks have the advantage of being relatively simple to invest in. Create an account with an online brokerage firm (such as Fidelity, Vanguard, E-TRADE, or Charles Schwab), click a few buttons, and purchase some stocks.

There will undoubtedly be some testing to be done along the way to ensure that you are making the best investments possible. I'm not recommending that you buy any stocks and then disregard them. However, remember the difference between purchasing stocks and purchase real estate or investing in a small business. Stocks can be traded quickly, easily, and cheaply, while real estate and many other assets cannot. Stocks often refer to as "liquid assets," which means that they can quickly transform into cash.

For instance, if you invested $1,000,000 in the market on a Tuesday at 3 p.m. and decided to cash out immediately, you can complete the transaction in a matter of minutes with a few mouse clicks.

An "illiquid asset," on the other hand, can take time and money to convert into cash. Consider owning a priceless painting. Finding the right buyer and selling your painting at a reasonable price will take weeks (possibly months) and money. Many people invest in stocks because it gives them the illusion that their money is never far away and can be called home at any time. According to research, this can be both a positive and a bad thing.

- **Invest in Stocks for Free Of Tax Profits**

The government provides various tax-free accounts that allow you to stop paying taxes on your assets legally. Tax avoidance will make a massive difference in the amount of money your investments gain over time. The greater the fantastic positive effect of avoiding taxes, the more money you raise and spend.

However, to benefit from these tax-free savings accounts, you must generally invest in stocks or similar assets (mutual funds or ETFs). You'll be losing out on a tremendous gift from the US government if you stay out of the stock market: decades and decades of tax-free investment growth.

- **To Save for Retirement, Invest in Stocks.**

Many people put money into their retirement accounts not only for the tax-free returns mentioned above but also to have a nice big nest egg to live off when they retire. You've probably heard it before (and I'll repeat it now, and probably ten more times): You can save a substantial sum of money for retired life if you start saving when you are still young. Tax-free savings accounts, as well as monthly deposits from your regular salary, help to fuel the growth of your investments. If you want to stop working at a point in the future and don't want to rely on social security to help you and your family, investing in stocks can be an excellent way to prepare for retirement.

- **For Consistent Income, Invest in Dividend Stocks**

Dividend stocks are special in that they pay you cash dividends every month. Depending on the dividend stock you purchase, you will receive cash payments ranging from 1% to 10% (and beyond) of your total investment each year.

Let's assume you buy a portfolio of 20 dividend stocks that collectively pay a dividend of 4% of your total investment. Assume you've just retired from a long and successful career and can invest $500,000 of your life savings in this portfolio.

Your dividend stock portfolio will pay you $20,000 in cash per year simply for owning it ($500,000 investment x 4% annual dividends = $20,000 per year).

Many dividends are collected per quarter, ensuring that $20,000 in dividends is paid in the year instead of one lump sum. That doesn't even consider the likelihood that those stocks will appreciate over time, allowing you to profit even more. Dividend stocks are common among retirees because they provide a constant stream of cash regardless of market fluctuations.

- **Diversify your portfolio by investing in stocks.**

Purchasing stocks help you to diversify your investments and revenue streams for yourself and your family. What exactly does "diversify" imply?

The even more opportunities you need to generate income, the much less likely you will encounter monetary difficulties if one of them fails.

Assume you have a full-time job, rent out an extra room in your house to a college student, do some handy work on weekends, and invest in dividend stocks.

You wouldn't lose any of your money if either of those sources of income dried up (for example, if you lost your full-time job or if you injured your back and couldn't do any handy work). Due to the income diversification provided by the additional room rental and dividend stocks, you could be able to withstand a difficult patch.

Investing follows the same principle. Investing in stocks will help you diversify your sources of income.

Maybe you have money set aside in your company's retirement plan, in a savings account, in CDs, or somewhere else. Stocks are another form of investment that can protect you from potential problems in a single sector.

- **Invest in stocks to own a piece of a company you admire.**

You become a part-owner of a business when you purchase even a single share. When you buy Apple (AAPL) stock, you become a shareholder in the business. As a result, Apple's CEO, Tim Cook, is legally your employee. Perhaps you have a deep connection to some brands and products and would like to own a piece of the business. Furthermore, this does not only make you feel fine, but it has another major advantage.

- **Invest in stocks to vote on important issues**

When you have stock in a firm, you are lawfully entitled to elect on major issues as an investor. Issues like a possible merger, the addition of a director to the board of directors, and even executive compensation packages may be licensed or declined.

As a shareholder, you're granted a "proxy vote," which allows you to vote on major issues that will resolve at the upcoming shareholder meeting remotely (usually electronically or by mail). If you care about a business, purchasing its stock is a great way to ensure that you have a say in some of its major decisions.

- **Invest in Stocks to Make Money from Industries You Are Familiar**

With

Peter Lynch, a well-known Fidelity investor, is known for his investment strategy of "invest in what you know."

The idea is that you're an expert in something, and you'll be able to make extremely wise investment decisions in that field. Suppose you work full-time as a dentist and discover a game-changing new dental technology that's sweeping the industry, for example. In that case, you might consider investing in the stock of that company.

As a dentist (or whatever your specialty is), you're in a unique position to recognize companies in your industry that are poised to expand. And if you buy their stock now, you'll be able to reap before others do. In reality, though, things aren't always so straightforward. Although it's a good idea to "cash in what you know" now and then, it shouldn't be your primary stock buying strategy. But now and then, you're in a rare position to see anything before anyone else. That's a brilliant way to make money.

- **Learn by Investing in Stocks**

Stock investing will teach you a lot. You'll understand more about the services, what drives their success or failure, you'll comprehend just how products are produced, and the impact of markets on organizations.

You'll also discover new ways of thinking. Investing in the stock market necessitates rationality, study, and careful consideration. Putting these skills to the test with investing would undoubtedly improve them in other areas of your life.

- **Have a Nice Time Trading in Stocks**

Stock investment is a lot of fun. You will have the ability to learn about businesses and products, judge CEOs and business executives, and make strategic decisions that will directly affect your financial future. There's nothing rather like getting stock and watching it increase up and up in time. When you reach your account, you'll see how much you've won, and you'll feel proud.

- **Takeaway**

Stock market investing is about learning, having fun, and making money.

But, believe it or not, it's about more than "making money." When done correctly, stock investment helps you make more money with less effort by using the money you already have.

Assume you have $10,000 to invest in the stock market. How long did it take you to gain $10,000? Remember that you most likely had to make a lot more than $10,000 to pay the taxman and then have $10,000 leftover. <u>For how long did it take you to complete the project?</u>:

Is it true that it took six months?

Is it only three months?

Is it only a month?

Is it just one week?

I'm guessing you put in a lot of effort to raise the $10,000, no matter how long it took. What if you could invest $10,000 in the stock market, do some analysis and trading on the side, and turn that $10,000 into $20,000 over ten years? What if, in other words, you could double your money in ten years?

Although the first $10,000 could have taken weeks or months of hard work, the $10,000 of market profit you made was gained while you were away doing other things.

When someone says, "Make your money work for you," they're referring to this. It's also what legendary businessman Warren Buffet had in mind when he said, "If you don't figure out how to make money while you sleep, you'll work until you die." You're working hard to earn $10,000 when your money is working hard to earn you an extra $10,000. And how quickly your money will earn the next $10,000 is determined by your investment skills. The quicker you get better at buying stocks, the more money you'll make.

Of course, it isn't always that straightforward. You can't just put your money in the stock market and expect it to rise independently. Along the way, there are many dangers, traps, and obstacles.

And not everybody is a good match for the stock market. To make your money grow over time, you'll need dedication, persistence, wise decisions, and consistent effort. If you skip either of those steps, you risk losing money in the stock market. However, I believe that the stock market is one of the best ways to increase your capital. You can also do it with very little effort on your part. It can be easy money if done correctly.

How to Make Money in Stocks

What is the key to making money in the stock market? Investing for the long haul in both good and poor times is how you do it.

The average annual return on the stock market is 10%, which is higher than that of a bank account or bonds. So, after investing in the stock market, why do so many people struggle to gain 10%? Many people may not invest for long enough.

The trick to earning money in stocks is to remain in the marketplace; your overall success is better predicted by your "time in the market." Unfortunately, investors often enter and exit the stock market at inopportune moments, thus missing out on the annual return. Keep investing in stocks if you want to make profits.

More time means more chances for your assets to increase in value. The best corporations' profits appear to grow over time, and investors reward these higher profits with a higher stock price. The higher price translates into a profit for the stock's owners. Before you can start saving, you'll need a brokerage account.

If the business pays dividends, having more time in the market helps you to earn them. You should kiss those dividends goodbye if you trade in and out of the market regularly, weekly, or monthly because you don't own the stock at the key points on the calendar to catch the payouts. Consider this if that isn't enough to persuade you. According to Putnam Investments, those who stayed fully invested in the business for the 15 years leading up to 2017 saw a 9.9% annual return.

However:

When you missed only ten of the best days during that period, your annual return plummeted to 5%.

If you skipped the best 20 days, your annual return fell to 2%.

You lost money if you skipped the 30 best days (-0.4 percent annually).

In other words, if you had stayed invested for just ten more important days, you would have won twice as much (and you wouldn't have had to control the market). No one can predict which days these will be, so investors must remain invested the whole time to take advantage of them. You'll get closer to the historical average annual return of 10% the longer you stay in.

How much money can I make in the securities market?

"How much money can I make from stocks?" is one of the most relevant stock market investing issues. Let's get straight to the point:

You can make a great deal of money in the stock exchange if you start early, save consistently, and invest sensibly; however, how much is a lot?

I discovered ten big insights on how much money you can make in the stock market after conducting extensive research:

1. Over long periods, stocks typically return 7–10 percent per year.

2. They could do much better or much worse in any given year.

3. The business almost always makes money over longer periods (10–15 years).

4. Dividend stocks are worth paying attention to because they account for about 40% of the stock market's returns (although it varies over time).

5. Individual investors can outperform or underperform the market, depending on how skilled they are at investing and whether they avoid popular pitfalls.

6. Your money will grow faster if you remain in the market for a longer period.

7. Your wealth will grow faster if your annual investment returns are higher.

8. Small increases in your investment returns will add to a substantial increase in your wealth over time.

9. Your wealth would grow faster if you can stop paying taxes on your investment gains.

10. Over long periods, solid stock investment returns compound to produce almost mystical sums of money.

What Is the Return on the Stock Market?

First, we must decide how high the stock market will rise (or fall) while investing.

The question of how much the stock market will return has sparked many studies, but also for this conversation, let's keep it very easy.

According to most analysts, the stock market has historically returned by 7% to 10% annually in the last 100 years.

When you've had an average return of 7% to 10% over several years, it's a long-term return. It's not what you should dream of seeing year after year.

For example, when the stock market collapsed in 2008, the S&P 500 (a list of the 500 largest companies on the market) returned a catastrophic -38.5 percent loss. The following year, it rebounded to a healthy +23.5 percent gain. Those are two extreme examples, and returns usually do not differ that much. It does, however, bring up a significant point:

The long-term performance of stocks yield 7% to 10% is reasonably stable, while stock market returns are highly volatile in the short term.

Isn't the Stock market risky?

Yeah, indeed. The stock market is extremely dangerous. <u>You'll have to deal with two forms of risks:</u>

1. The market's inherent risk, and;

2. Ignorance risk

- **Inherent Risk in the Market:** This risk exists because it is difficult to predict a stock price completely 100 percent of the time. According to one of the forecasting principles, the more accurate a prediction is, the more likely it is to be incorrect (making intelligent predictions). In the sense that more general predictions are more likely to be accurate, the reverse is also true. It means that a forecast that the stock price will increase by 10% tomorrow is more likely to be inaccurate than predicting that the stock price will increase by 10% for the next two years. It is why short-term investing is considered riskier than long-term investing. The stock market is inherently risky since it can never predict the exact value of your investment. The good news is that this risk level is appropriate if you consider the possibility of being incorrect. This form of risk can be easily handled by diversification and other investment strategies.

- On the other hand, when an investor expects that his forecast will be right, the inherent risk becomes a major issue. If he believes there is no risk of making a mistake, the investor is unlikely to have made any preparations if he is incorrect. There is a much more dangerous form of risk to be mindful of: the risk of ignorance.

- **Ignorance Risk:** One of my favorite quotes on investing by Robert Kiyosaki sums up the risk of ignorance perfectly. "It's not the investment that's risky; it's the investor." Completely understanding this quote means that investments have little to no risk. There are only two types of investments: good and poor. The danger occurs when the investor is unable to differentiate between the two. When I first read the quote, I was completely amazed. I had to read it many times because it contradicted one of the most basic investing principles: "high risk, high reward." If Robert Kiyosaki was right, it meant that he could achieve higher returns without taking on greater risks. All you had to do was become a more savvy investor. It was perplexing but inspiring at the same time. With more study, I came across the following passage from

Benjamin Graham's book "The Intelligent Investor": "It has long been an old and sound theory that those who cannot afford to take risks should be comfortable with a low return on their invested funds." As a result, the general notion has established that the return rate an investor can aim for is more or less proportional to the level of risk he is willing to take. Our point of view differs. The optimal return rate should be calculated by how much intelligent effort the investor is willing and able to put into his mission. Our passive investor, who seeks both protection and freedom from worry, receives the minimum return. The attentive and shrewd investor who exactly knows what they are doing would see the best return." I felt fantastic after reading this. It felt amazing to know that stock market success wasn't dependent on luck. Instead, disciplined research relied on it.

What amount of money should I invest in stocks?

When young people first start investing in the stock market, they often have two types of "how much money" questions:

1. To begin investing, what sum should I invest in stocks?

2. Can I spend a certain amount of money on stocks?

These are two entirely separate inquiries. "To begin a stock investment, how much money do I need?" It is about the bare minimum needed to begin investing. On the other hand, "how much money can I put into stocks?" Is concerned about how much of your savings should be invested in the stock market. Let's take a look at each one individually.

- **How Much Money Do I Require to Begin Investing in Stocks?**

In theory, there is no set amount of money required to begin investing in stocks. However, you'll most likely need at least $200 to $1,000 to get started properly. To open an account and begin buying stocks, most brokerages have no minimum requirements. So, in theory, you could open an account with just $1 today.

However, three variables serve as a natural floor for the amount of money you can begin investing with. You can, in general, have enough money to:

Buy a single stock share.

Make sure your portfolio is well diversified.

Keep your income safe from trading commissions.

Let's inspect each of these and then figure out how you can circumvent them if you're a beginner.

To buy a single share of stock, you'll need enough money

Even though many brokers allow you to open an account with just $1, the question remains: "What stock can you buy for $1?"

There are plenty of penny stocks that sell for less than a dollar, but I wouldn't start there. Instead, you'll want to buy a stock (or multiple stocks) based on your study. To begin investing, you'll need enough money to buy at least one share, which can cost anything from $1 to $300,000.

There is, however, a relatively new solution to this problem. Investors can purchase fractional shares for as little as $5 from a few brokerage startups. You might, for example, purchase $5 worth of Amazon instead of $1,823 for a single share.

While I haven't used Stash's facilities, there might be some worth considering.

You'll Need Enough Money to Diversify Your Portfolio Properly

Another thing to bear in mind when beginning is that you must shop enough stocks (in various positions) to be sufficiently diversified

Simply put, you can aspire to own between 10 and 30 positions. If you have $1,000 to spend, I'm not recommending you break it up into ten different places. It's fine to start with a small number of positions, particularly if you intend to add more later.

I'd recommend buying a different stock with the next $1,000 and a third stock with the $1,000 after that when you add money to your savings account.

You should avoid putting all of your capital into a single stock because this will result in you being excessively concentrated and binding your entire investment future to one position.

If you're starting with a greater sum of money (say, $20,000 or more), you may want to start with a portfolio of ten positions ($2,000 per position). Whatever the starting point, bear in mind that you want to reach as much healthy diversity as possible as soon as possible.

To protect your income from trading fees, you'll need enough money

Trading costs are another factor to consider. Trading fees will eat into your income if you start with a small amount of money in your investment account. Consider the following scenario.

Assume you have just $100, to begin with. You spend $100 on a single stock and immediately pay a $5 trading fee. The stock then rises in value by $10, and you sell it for a $5 trading fee. Unfortunately, trading fees wiped out your profit. You began with $100, lost $5 in trading fees right away, earned $10 when the stock rose, and then paid another $5 in trading fees. You were able to keep the initial $100.

Another way to look at it is that if you purchased a stock for $100, you were immediately down 10% on your investment because you had to overcome $10 in trading costs before you could make a profit. Fees now detract this much from earnings when you spend small sums of money. A pair of $5 trading fees will only decrease your profit by 0.2 percent if you invested $5,000 or more. It's not a big deal.

If you spend less than $1,000, on the other hand, you'll be down 1% or more before your stock has even had a chance to move. If you intend to spend more than $5,000, any major online broker should suffice. The majority of them charge between $5 and $7 per exchange, and they're constantly lowering their rates. However, if your initial investment is less than $5,000 (which is perfectly fine), you might intend to look for a broker that offers free trades.

- **What Is the Appropriate Amount of Money to Invest in Stocks?**

Let's turn our attention to the second question: How much of your money should you put into the stock market? I attempt to put however much as could reasonably be expected in the financial exchange because the extraordinary influence of compounding can deliver huge wealth over the long haul. Any additional dollar you put into the market wisely today may be worth $5, $10, $20, or more in the future.

However, there are a few main guidelines I follow to keep my stock market investment to a minimum:

Never spend so much money that your financial future is jeopardized, and never invest money you will use in the next 5–10 years.

Never spend so much money that you can't get a good night's sleep.

Let's observe each of these:

- **Don't Put Your Financial Future at Risk**

Don't take any chances that could put your financial future in jeopardy. Yes, seeing all of your capital compoundings in the market is appealing. But bear in mind that it's not uncommon for markets to drop by 50% or more in a single year. And some investors may lose all of their money in the market due to poor investment decisions or bad luck.

On Wall Street, there's an old saying: "Bulls make money, bears make money, pigs get slaughtered."

- Bulls — investors who believe the market is going up — make money over time;

- Bears — financial backers who believe the market will fall — bring in cash over time;

- However, pigs — eager, restless, and excessively risky financial backers — are slaughtered.

When it comes to trading in the stock market, it's not the place to take chances. But never spend so much of your money that a -50 percent (or more) drop will wipe out your savings.

Or, in the words of famous investor Warren Buffet, "You should not be in the stock market unless you can watch your stock holdings fall by 50% without being panicked."

Don't put money into investments that you won't need in the next 5–10 years

Another investment advice piece is never to spend money you will use shortly (typically the next 5–10 years). What is the reason for this? There are many explanations for this.

Second, stocks will drop dramatically during market downturns, reducing the amount of capital you have available. Let's presume you have $30,000 to invest in the market and expect to purchase a new home in two years. You invest $30,000 in some great value stocks, but the S& P 500 drops -60% in two years due to a bear market. Your value stocks have only dropped -50 percent (much better than the market), but you only have $15,000 to put down on the house. You may have to put your new home purchase on hold.

It is why investors advise only investing in markets where you can expect a -50 percent drop in value and won't need to sell anytime soon.

The final point you need to do is buy bigger, consider the rate loss by 50%, and then withdraw your capital from the market at its lowest stage, just before it begins a long and prosperous recovery. Another reason to stop spending money in the market that you'll need in the next 5–10 years is that you don't want to be pressured to sell before you're ready.

Let's say you do a lot of research and decide to invest in a good value stock. It rises 10% to your delight, and it appears to be on the rise again. However, because you require the funds for something other than saving, you are required to sell your stock and forfeit future profits. It may result in you receiving a tax bill on your capital gains earlier than anticipated.

Don't bring money into the stock market you'll need in cash in the next 5–10 years

Don't put too much money into anything that you can't sleep at night. If you've put so much money into the market that any little dip and correction keeps you up at night, you've either spent too much or stock market investing isn't for you. Now, I'm not saying you shouldn't worry about your savings or keep track of them—quite the opposite, in reality.

However, you don't want your investments to cause you a lot of anxiety. It's unhealthy, and it'll lead you to make poor investment decisions based on emotion and paranoia rather than logic.

Takeaway

"Just get started," I will advise most new investors.

There's a long way to go about putting resources into the stock market, and it's useful to experience the fundamentals with less cash on the line. What matters more than the amount you put in today is how many you add over time. For several factors, gradually growing your savings over time is likely to result in a substantial increase in your long-term wealth. Start with what you have now and gradually add more capital, positions, and strategies as you learn more about what works best for you.

<u>Also, keep in mind the following main points:</u>

There is no minimum investment to begin investing, but you would most likely need at least $200 to $1,000 to get started properly.

If you have less than $1,000 to invest, it's fine to start with only one stock and gradually increase your holdings.

If you're just getting started, some brokerages will let you buy partial shares for $5 or make free trades.

I try to put as much money into stocks as possible because every dollar I put into stocks today might be worth $5, $10, $20, or more in the future.

However, you can never put money into stocks you would use in the next 5–10 years.

Never take undue risks or spend so much money that the whole financial situation is jeopardized.

Isn't it true that I have to have a million dollars before I can start investing?

Your finances, wages, debt, and monthly expenses will decide how much you can save before investing. Until the vast majority start saving, they should take care of any high-interest obligation and put to the side at any rate three months of costs in a just-in-case account.

Emergency funds are a way to put money together for the unforeseeable financial crises that life throws at you. Bills can pile up quickly, from broken-down vehicles to unexpected accidents or illnesses. An emergency fund will also prevent you from losing your job or being laid off unexpectedly.

If you've covered those bases, you'll likely be in a decent spot to start investing a portion of your money. To begin saving, you don't need $10,000. You don't even need $100 to get started. At many big brokerages, you can get started investing for less than $10. You can also spend as little as $5 with fractional shares and commission-free stock and ETF trades.

Focusing on large index funds with low management fees might be a good strategy if you start with a small portfolio. S&P 500 ETFs, which screen the yield of 500 of the country's biggest stocks, typically have yearly charges of under 0.10 percent and are upheld by fractional investing.

You should diversify into additional funds and consider other, more concentrated investments as you can afford to add more to your portfolio.

Investing isn't just for the rich people

For many people who wanted to invest in the past, working with a stockbroker to buy and sell stocks was prohibitively costly. Investing is now more available than ever, thanks to a combination of no fees, support for fractional shares, and the opportunity to invest through mobile apps.

You presumably have enough set aside to begin saving if you have a base backup stash and have taken care of high-interest debt like Visas.

Isn't it exhausting?

Stress and danger are inextricably linked. You're a stressed investor if you're a risky investor—the sensation of being out of control and unsure of what to do next causes stress. And not knowing what to do next stems from a lack of knowledge about a lack of study. Consider two Calculus students taking an examination. Student A prepared for the exam for several weeks. Student B had just recently begun studying the night before. Who do you think would be more depressed in the days leading up to, during, and after the exam? Let's apply the previous example to the stock market. Rick just got word that one of his coworkers, Steve, made $3000 in one day on the stock market. He sought more information from a friend and requested that he remind him of the next big thing in the stock market. Rick's friend tells him that he can double his money in a week if he invests in XYZ Business. Rick is overjoyed by the news and invests his $10000 savings in XYZ the same day. Rick checks his account the next day and discovers that he only has $9000 in his account. He presses his friend for an explanation. His friend laughs at him and assures him that it will heal on its own. His friend tells him to review his account in a week when it would have doubled. Rick, who is a very trusting person, takes the advice. He opens his account a week later, and his account balance is $1000. In only one week, he lost 90% of his savings. Consider the burden Rick was under. He blamed his friend for his financial losses and vowed never to invest in the stock market again. Rick was unprepared and took a lot of chances as a result of his inexperience. Because of the stress, I'm sure he can't sleep at night. Prepare if you don't want to be stressed. That's what there is to it.

How do I start investing in the stock market?

If you're ready to start investing in the stock market but aren't sure where to begin, this section will guide you.

It could come as an astonishment to hear that a $10,000 interest in the S&P 500 file 50 years prior is currently worth almost $1.2 million. When done correctly, stock investment is one of the most successful ways to create long-term wealth. We'll show you how to do it.

Before you dive in, there's a lot you should remember. Here's a step-by-step guide to stock market investing so you can make sure you're doing it correctly.

Below is a bit by bit manual for beginning with stock investing:

Decide on your investing approach.

Decide how much money you'll put into stocks.

Open an investment account.

Invest in a variety of stocks.

Continue to invest

- **Decide on your investment strategy**

The main consideration is how to get started with stock investing. Some investors prefer to purchase individual stocks, while others prefer to be more passive.

Try this exercise:

One of the accompanying assertions most precisely depicts you?

- I'm an analytical individual and appreciate doing math and doing research.

- I fear math and dislike doing a lot of "homework."

- I have several hours per week to invest in the stock market.

- I enjoy reading about various businesses that I might invest in, but I'm not interested in learning anything about math.

- I'm a working professional with little time to learn how to evaluate stocks.

The good news is that you can still become a stock market investor regardless of which of these claims you agree with. The "how" is the only thing that can change.

The numerous stock market investment options

- **Individual stocks:** If you have the time and ability to analyze and review stocks regularly thoroughly, you should invest in individual stocks. If this is the case, we strongly advise you to do so. A wise and patient investor has a good chance of outperforming the market over time. If quarterly earnings results and modest statistical estimates, on the other hand, don't appeal to you, there's nothing wrong with taking a more passive approach.

- **Index funds:** You can invest in index funds, which follow a stock index such as the S&P 500, in addition to purchasing individual stocks. When it comes to actively managed funds or passively managed funds, we prefer the latter (although there are certainly exceptions). Index funds have lower fees and are always expected to approximate the long-term performance of their underlying indexes. The S&P 500 has delivered total returns of about 10% annualized over time, and such output can create significant wealth over time.

- **Robo-advisors:** Last but not least, the Robo-advisor has grown in popularity in recent years. A Robo-advisor is a brokerage that invests your money on your behalf in an index fund portfolio customized to your age, risk tolerance, and investment objectives. A Robo-advisor will not only choose your investments, but many can also maximize your tax efficiency and make adjustments automatically over time.

Here are a few terms to be aware of:

Index Funds: This common investment vehicle mimics a stock index's performance and can help you balance your portfolio.

ETFs: ETFs, or exchange-traded funds, offer limited market exposure and trade similarly to stocks.

Mutual Funds: Low-fee passive mutual funds may provide great exposure to many stocks at once.

Bonds: Like most individuals borrow money from time to time, businesses and municipalities borrow money by bonds.

- **Decide how much money you'll put into stocks.**

Although the stock market would almost certainly grow in the long run, there is just so much volatility in stock prices in the short term — a drop of 20% in a single year is not uncommon. The stock market decreased by more than 40% during the COVID-19 pandemic in 2020, until its all-time high in months. Let's start with the money you shouldn't put into stocks.

At the very least, the stock market is not a good place to put money that you might use in the next five years. As a result, stop investing in the following:

- Your emergency fund account
- Money for your child's next tuition payment
- Money for next year's holiday fund
- Money is put aside for a down payment, even though you won't be able to purchase a house for many years.

Asset allocation

Let's talk about what you can do with your investable capital, which is money you won't use in the next five years. Asset allocation is the term for this concept, and it includes a few variables. Your age, as well as your risk tolerance and investment goals, are essential considerations to consider.

Let's begin by looking at your age. The overall thought is that as you get older, stocks become less engaging as a shelter for your pay. If you're young, you'll have decades to ride out any market ups and downs, but if you're retired and relying on your retirement income, this isn't the case.

Here's a straightforward, dependable guideline to help you discover what your asset allocation ought to be. Subtract your age from 110. What you get will be a rough approximation of the number of your investable funds that should be invested in stocks (this includes mutual funds and ETFs that are stock-based). The balance should be invested in fixed-income instruments such as bonds or high-yield certificates of deposit. You can then change this ratio to meet your risk tolerance. Consider the following scenario: you are 40 years old. According to this guideline, you can invest 70 percent of your available funds in stocks and the remaining 30 percent in fixed income. You might need to change this proportion for stocks if you're a daring person or hope to work past the normal retirement age. If you don't like major swings in your portfolio, on the other hand, you may want to move it in the opposite direction.

Open an investment account.

All of the stock buying for beginners' advice in the world won't benefit you if you don't have a way to buy stocks. To do that, you'll need a brokerage account, which is a specialized form of account.

Companies like TD Ameritrade, E-Trade, Charles Schwab, and others have these accounts. In most situations, opening a brokerage account is an easy and painless procedure that takes just a few minutes. You can conveniently finance your brokerage account through an EFT transfer, a check, or a wire transfer. Opening a brokerage account is usually easy, but there are a few items to consider before selecting a broker:

Type of account

Think about how much money market fund you want first. Most people only learn how to invest in the stock market, which means deciding between a traditional investment account and an individual retirement account (IRA). You can buy stocks, mutual funds, and ETFs with any account form. The key things to consider are why you're investing in stocks and how quickly you'd like to access your assets. You'll probably want a regular brokerage account if you want quick access to your assets, are just saving for a rainy day, or want to spend more than the annual IRA cap.

On the other hand, an IRA is a perfect way to build up a retirement nest egg if your goal is to prepare for retirement. Traditional and Roth IRAs are the most common types, but some specialized IRAs for self-employed individuals and small business owners, such as the SEP-IRA and SIMPLE IRA.

Compare Costs and features

Trading fees have been eliminated by most online stock brokers, putting most (yet not all) on a level battleground regarding prices.

There are, however, several significant variations. Some brokers, for example, provide customers with a range of educational resources, investment analysis, and other features that are particularly beneficial to new investors. Others allow you to trade on international stock exchanges. Some also have physical branch networks, which can be useful if you need personal investment advice.

There's also the broker's trading platform's user-friendliness and accessibility to remember. I've used a couple of them and can tell you that some are significantly more "clunky" than others. Many will allow you to attempt a demo adaptation before you purchase, and if that is the situation, I unequivocally encourage you to do as such.

Choose your stocks

If you're looking for some great beginner-friendly investing ideas now that we've answered the question of how to buy stock, here are five great stocks to get you started.

Of course, <u>I can't cover everything you should think about when selecting and evaluating stocks in just a few paragraphs, but here are the key concepts to understand before you begin:</u>

Make your portfolio more diverse.

Invest only in companies that you are familiar with.

Once you've had the hang of investing, stay away from high-volatility securities.

Avoid penny stocks no matter what.

Understand the fundamental metrics and principles used to evaluate stocks.

It's a good idea to understand the principle of diversification, which means that your portfolio can include many different types of companies. However, I would advise against over-diversification. Stick to industries you're familiar with, and if you discover you're good at (or comfortable with) assessing a specific form of stock, there's nothing wrong with that industry accounting for a sizable portion of your portfolio.

Purchasing ostentatious high-growth stocks may appear to be a phenomenal method to make abundance (and it very well, maybe). Yet, I'd encourage you to stand by until you're somewhat more experienced before doing as such. It's safer to build a "foundation" for your portfolio with well-established companies.

If you want to invest in individual securities, you can learn how to test them using some of the most common methods. A decent spot to begin is with this guide to esteem investing. It will help you in discovering stocks with appealing valuations. This guide to growth investing is an incredible spot to begin if you need to add some energizing long-haul growth freedoms to your portfolio.

Continue to invest

Warren Buffett, the Oracle of Omaha, shares one of the most important investment secrets. You don't have to do something special to produce extraordinary results. Warren Buffett is not only the world's most active long-term investor but also one of the strongest sources of investment advice.

Buying shares in great companies at fair rates and keeping them for as long as the businesses stay great is the most surefire way to make money in the stock market (or until you need the money). You'll have some uncertainty along the way if you do this, but you'll end up with outstanding investment returns in the long run.

What are the most popular investment strategies?

One of the most critical financial choices an investor makes is selecting the best investment strategy.

Your investment plan ought to mirror your conditions, investing periods, and hazard resistance as a confided guide to your monetary objectives. As a result, the "best" investment strategy can vary from person to person.

I go through eight traditional investment strategies in this section of the book. If you were to understand each aspect, you would have a well-informed option of strategies to choose from. I recommend looking for guidance from an authorized monetary consultant before settling on any speculation choices to guarantee your arrangement is custom-fitted to your particular necessities.

1. Fundamental Analysis

Fundamental analysis seeks to assess an asset's intrinsic value – that is, what its price should be compared to the current market price – by examining economic and financial variables that can influence its value. This data is gathered from publicly accessible data of a company, such as financial statements and the market in which it operates. Analysts equate the asset or stock's intrinsic value to its market price to assess if it is undervalued or overvalued and then suggest investing accordingly.

2. Value Investing

Value investing is a long-term investment approach in which investors use fundamental analysis to find assets or securities that the market has undervalued and purchase them at a discount. This strategy is based on the assumption that investors overreact to news, resulting in short-term volatility in demand and market price, even though the asset's intrinsic value remains unchanged. This overreaction encourages investors to buy cheap and profit when the market returns to normal, and the intrinsic value is recognized.

3. Growth Investing

Growth investors put resources into assets or securities that have a high potential for future capital growth and are projected to ascend faster than the market all in all. Long or short-term capital appreciation – dividends earned when sold rather than distributions obtained while owned – is the aim of growth investing. As a result, this strategy isn't recommended for investors looking for a steady stream of income. Growth investors weigh several factors when determining whether or not to invest, including the asset's current state, market prospects, and growth potential.

4. Technical Evaluation

Unlike fundamental analysis, which decides the value of an investment or asset based on internal factors such as sales and borrowings, technical analysis employs charts to forecast future patterns and trends based on recent market behavior, such as price shifts, trading rates, and volatility. Investors can predict future trends and invest accordingly by identifying those cues and signals, known as indicators.

5. Investing in Income

With global cash rates at historical lows, producing significant cash flow from investments is becoming more difficult. The point of pay investing is to make an enhanced speculation portfolio that creates reliable pay. Dividends, fund returns, bond yields, and interest payments are all examples of sources of profits. Income investors frequently consider factors such as yield, past performance stability, growth, and earnings to decide if a potential investment is a good match for their portfolio. Real estate portfolios, shares, mutual funds, land funds or trusts, and bonds are examples of these investments.

6. Investing in Buy and Hold

Purchase and Hold is a long haul, passive investment procedure in which investors purchase an asset or stock and hold it for an all-encompassing timeframe, paying little heed to market fluctuations. This investment strategy is based on the hypothesis that a longer-term investment will yield a higher return than a short-term investment. Investors who buy and hold deliberately pick stocks but are unconcerned with short-term volatility or technical indicators.

7. Sustainable Investing

Sustainable investors tend to make investments with positive social implications. Investing in funds or companies that promote social justice and environmental protection may be preferable to funds or companies that promote gambling and addiction. Sustainable investment also acknowledges that the businesses tackling the world's most urgent problems are frequently well-positioned for expansion. However, due to the essence of investing, long-term investors need to understand their investments' financial prospects in addition to their social importance.

8. Dollar-Cost Averaging

Dollar-cost averaging is a long-term investment technique that seeks to reduce market volatility's effect on the investment. Rather than trying to time the market and buying in an asset or stock all at once, investors in this approach buy smaller, fixed amounts at regular intervals over time. As a result, investors pay a more "normal" purchase price over the entire investment period, as the asset's price will always fluctuate with each investment.

How to Choose the Best Investing Strategy

There are far more investment strategies than those listed in this book. There are far too many to list. When you make an informed decision based on your financial situation, any of these strategies can generate a significant return. They all accompany their arrangement of dangers that ought to consider painstakingly. It would help if you had an investment strategy, regardless of which one you choose.

Often consult a licensed financial advisor or financial planner when designing your investment strategy or making a significant investment decision. They will collaborate with you to create a plan that meets your requirements. <u>The following will help you choose the best investing strategy:</u>

- **Think like a Geek:** It is insufficient to rely solely on strategies. When you plan to make a profit, you should implement the best practices used by active investors. Adequate research It's understandable why so many people lose money when investing in stocks. Even though books on the topic stress the importance of conducting research, only a few people can conduct proper research. Lamentably, numerous investors accept that just exploring the market for two hours would furnish them with enough data to settle on a sound investment decision. It is incorrect. Be certain that you have done enough research. Research should be a natural part of your day-to-day life if you are serious about being a good investor. Begin little. It has no connection to the amount of money you have in your records. When you're a novice, it's best to start small. In reality, it is recommended that you start with a demo account to test the waters without putting any money on the line. It will also allow you to learn how to use your broker's platform properly. Often begin with a small move. You aim to become acquainted with the actual process of buying and selling stocks and formulate a winning strategy. Don't worry; once you've developed a solid plan, you can still increase your investment, thus increasing your potential benefit.

- **Diversification:** Perhaps the best way to will your risks is to diversify your investments. As they claim, do not put all your eggs in a basket. The explanation for this is that studying the stock market can only improve our chances of success. However, it can never guarantee a positive profit return. In reality, there's a risk you'll lose money on your investment. Stock investing, like any other successful investment opportunity, comes with risks. You will reduce your risk and mitigate your losses by diversifying your investments. You can achieve diversification in several ways. The most popular method is to buy stocks from various companies rather than investing all of your money in one. Another choice is to diversify the portfolio by sector. Industries rise and fall, and you do not influence this. By tomorrow, an industry that is thriving today will no longer be considered a viable investment. As a result, diversify your investments through industries. **Diversification by asset class** is another way to diversify. It is accomplished by investing in various asset classes, such as shares, stocks, commodities, etc. When using this technique, you must master the art of timing. Assets, for example, could be your best asset to invest in if the economy recovers. However, in a recession, investing in bonds could be a safer choice than stocks.

Diversification of strategies is another effective way to reduce risk. Such strategies could be more appropriate than others depending on where you want to invest or how you want to invest (short-term or long-term). In the case of a long-term investment, for example, financial analysis is an absolute must. Technical research can be one of the best methods to use when making a short-term investment. You may also pursue regional diversification. Many investors are skewed and only invest in businesses that are based in a specific region. Keep in mind that no industry in a particular geographic area will consistently outperform others. In the stock market, there are ups and downs. You may also vary the amount of time. It's important to remember that you don't have to spend your entire account balance in one day. You have the option of spreading your savings out over time. For instance, you could invest 20% of your money today and then another 30% the following month. Proper timing, like everything else in the industry, is crucial to success. Diversifying your investment means not putting all of your eggs in one basket. It's important to consider that diversification isn't the only way to make money. Choosing where to diversify and spend your capital is an essential aspect of diversification. As a result, you cannot overlook the significance of doing research and study.

- **Try not to follow Expert Advice all the time:** When you are an amateur, you may think that it's accommodating to scan the net for suggestions coming from the purported "experts." Since not all of these "experts" are true experts, this is a common blunder. It is pretty simple to spread a message and promote oneself online these days. A good stock marketer projects an investment portfolio image even though they have never purchased or sold a single share of stock. It's also worth remembering that even the most experienced experts make errors now and then. Developing your view of the stock market is the best way to stop relying on experts. After all, the difference between an expert and a total novice is that an expert has his perspective on the stock market and can defend it with sound arguments. At the same time, a beginner normally relies on what other people think. It doesn't discredit the significance of perusing or tuning in to what experts need to say. Rather, this means that you should treat any message or piece of advice with caution. Rather than focusing solely on what experts have to say, you may use their opinions as additional support for your investment plan.

- **Take note of the pump and dump scheme:** Pump and dump schemes are popular, and you should be aware of them. Tragically, even though numerous individuals know about the trick, numerous individuals get bulldozed. So, how does it function? A corporation or person that owns stocks promotes them and spreads positive rumors about them. It is a marketing gimmick that exaggerates the stock's value. It is likely to increase interest in the stocks. As a result, the price of the stocks will rise. When this occurs, other investors will offer to purchase the stocks, believing them to be a good investment. After the stock sales, the marketing and poor rumors will come to an end. After that, the stock prices will start to fall. After all, the real value of the stocks is smaller than their actual value or price. As a result, the stocks' seller earns a profit, while the buyer owns stock with an uncontrollable price decline. It's worth noting that the pump-and-dump system isn't inherently negative.

As you can see, you can benefit from it if you take advantage of it. The trick is to buy the stocks before or right after the pump and dump scheme's initial phase. You must then sell them just as their value starts to dwindle. When you see the slightest rise in benefit, the easiest and most basic solution is to sell the stocks. Do not wait for the campaign to end before acting. After all, you have no power over it. Stocks should not be kept for an extended period. It's worth remembering that not all investors lose money as a result of poor stock selection. Some people lose money when they invest in the right stocks but keep them for too long. Do not underestimate the stock market's uncertainty. Please make sure you sell your stocks until they fall in value. Please take advantage of the situation while it lasts.

- **Recognize the Concept of Volatility:** You should have a firm grasp of the concept of uncertainty. Many people associate volatility with stock prices that rise and fall at a seemingly random pace. They often believe that after a significant increase, a significant decline is to be predicted, and vice versa. It isn't always the case, however. If that were the case, uncertainty would be a simple thing to forecast. The stock market's volatility is affected by several factors. It means that even after a major decline in stock prices, another drop is still likely. It also implies that the outcome of a new exchange is unaffected by prior trades or transactions. Unfortunately, some people believe that since their previous three investments failed, the next trade would almost certainly succeed if they use the same technique. However, it is incorrect. In reality, there's a fair chance the next trade or investment will be a loss as well. The explanation for this is due to the technique you are employing. If your plan continues to lose, it is a warning that you can alter or at the very least adjust it. True professional investors don't put their trust in chance. They understand that if they can come up with a true winning plan, their chances of making money are high. It's imperative to recollect that even though you have a strong arrangement, there's consistently a danger you'll lose money. After all, no plan can guarantee a profit return of one hundred percent of the time. However, with consistent analysis, hard work, and practice, you can sway the odds in your favor and gain a competitive advantage over the stock market.

- **Maintain a Trading Journal:** Keeping a trading journal is not necessary, but it can be helpful. You don't need to be a competent writer to keep a trading journal, so don't be bothered. <u>You will, however, need two things:</u>

1. One, you must be truthful. It implies that you should be honest about your strengths and weaknesses, as well as the results of any investment you make.

2. Second, you must keep your journal up to date regularly.

Your trading journal will contain any information relevant to your life as an investor that you like. Ideally, you can write down your reasons for wanting to invest in stocks, as well as your short- and long-term objectives, in your report. You can refer to something in the future if you get lost or confused on your journey. Your plans, finances, and goals should all be recorded in your journal. Simply put, you make your journal as important as you want it to be. It is suggested that you fill your journal with as much detail as possible. The reason for this is that your journal allows you to see yourself in a different light. It will be simpler for you to recognize any blemishes or parts of your arrangement that should change. Your journal will advise you on a range of topics. Again, the most important thing is that you be absolutely honest in your journal and update it regularly.

- **Investing should not be seen as a pastime:** The unfortunate reality is that most people who invest in stocks do so as hobbies. Although you are free to treat it as a mere hobby, you should expect a rational outcome, just as you would if you treated any other company as a mere hobby with no engagement or dedication. Just in the unlikely event that you would need a steady income flow from your investment, treat it like a business or professional organization. The issue with the individuals who consider this sort of business just a leisure activity is that they don't invest the fundamental exertion and investigation in improving their odds of making a profit. The only way to deal with the stock market is often to sit it out. It is unavoidable that you will soon find yourself in a situation where the market is simply declining. Wait it out instead of getting too worked up and making risky investments. Waiting it out does not suggest that you can neglect the market entirely. It means you can keep an eye on what's going on in the market but refrain from making any moves or investments. Act only when the time is right. If the economy starts to rebound, make sure you're able to take advantage of it.

- **Be a trader who isn't emotional:** While it is important to be passionate about what you do, you should not let your emotions or passion affect your judgment. It is not enough to feel good and secure about an investment when you make one. Instead, you should be secure in your trade because you've done your homework and testing, and there are compelling reasons to believe it's the best investment. You won't be able to think if you let your emotions cloud your judgment. Consequently, if you feel your feelings interfere with your decision-making, you can pause and refrain from making any investment. Before you make a move, wait for the excessive emotion to fade away.

- **Take advantage of the bull market:** The stock market is defined as being in a bull market. It means that stock prices are rising in the economy, which is a positive thing. A bear or bearish market, on the other hand, is one in which prices are declining. A bull market is something you can learn to take advantage of. Essentially, the crucially important factor here is knowing when a bull market is underway or about to begin. It will help if you put your positions (investments) as soon as possible to benefit from the increase in stock prices. After a bear market, a bull market typically emerges. It is important that you know when a bear market ends and a bull market starts as soon as possible. To do so, you'll need to remain on top of your regular research and study. While a bull market can be reported on television, the best way to benefit from it is to invest right before it starts. Since a bear market normally accompanies a bull market, this is the case. It will already be too late for you if you wait for a bull market to be declared before acting. Remember that the best way to beat the stock market is to beat the opposition. Be the first to take every opportunity that comes your way.

- **Test and Develop your Strategy:** Always test your system and test it on numerous occasions before using it with genuine money. Observe that you need to rehash this interaction regardless of whether you change or change a minor piece of your technique. Using a trial account or paying the minimum sum is a safe way to do this. When you're first starting, you should devote a considerable amount of time to creating a solid plan that will benefit you. It is recommended that you concentrate on improving your success rate. Keep in mind that your primary goal as a beginner is not to make money right away. Your primary goal ought to be to define a triumphant arrangement. Of course, a winning strategy is contingent on the circumstances and the amount of research you do. When it comes to stock market success, the more knowledge you have, the more likely you will make the right investment. Take your time. It takes time to figure out which investment is the best.

- **Never Pursue Your Losses:** This is a popular piece of gambling advice: don't chase your losses. The majority of people who chase after their losses are well aware of this advice, which is very shocking. Despite knowing that chasing after one's losses is not a good practice, they continue to fall into this trap. After a major loss, investors are often tempted to chase their losses. You really cannot think clearly after a major setback. Thus, despite your awareness that it's useless, you might be tempted to press on and regain what you've lost. You would almost definitely lose all of your money in the end. As a result, to avoid losing leverage, make sure you have the strength to stop making any investment if you experience a major loss. Allow yourself a period to forget about the stock market. People typically attempt to make up for their losses by making a greater investment in the hopes of restoring their losses and still making a profit. After all, they've already put in some effort and time. The trick is to stay calm and reflect on your winnings rather than on what you have already lost. Keep in mind that each investment you make is distinct from the others.

• As a result, when you experience a setback, confess and embrace it and move on. After all, even the best plan in the world can occasionally struggle. The most important thing is that you end up with a positive profit when you sum it up. Only put money into investments that you can afford to lose. Another piece of gambling advice is to play with money that you can afford to lose. Even though you will not be gambling, you must keep in mind that this is a financial investment. And, as in any other savings, there's a risk you won't make any money or even lose it all. As a result, you should not use money that you need to pay for your commitments, such as money for household expenses, to be sure. Borrowing money from others is often not a good idea. It is to save you from being buried in debt if the worst happens. If you need additional financial assistance, you may form a partnership with another individual.

• **Never give up:** Also, the best stock investors have their share of bad luck. They have a long history of losing money in the stock market. They are, however, the ones who have triumphed over the obstacles and dominated the race. You will face various challenges as you progress and spend more time investing in stocks. What counts is that you don't give up and that you learn from your mistakes. You are not at odds with the stock market. It's a profit goldmine for you. Your only opponent is you. It would help if you upheld a high degree of professionalism and discipline. When you're going through a tough patch, stay calm and give yourself time to heal. Do not surrender. Unwind. Allow yourself to relax. It's very simple to get dependent on the stock market, especially when profits begin to come in. You must, however, allow yourself time to unwind. Know that allowing your mind to relax will help you make better investment decisions. Also, making a substantial profit in the stock market takes time. As a consequence, take some time to relax now and then return to work better.

CHAPTER 7
Trading Psychology Of Millionaire Investors

What's the most significant distinction between you and millionaire investors?

You are mistaken if you believe it is the sum of money you have. The most important distinction is in how you think. Most millionaires aren't ordinary citizens who happen to come with a huge amount of money. Instead, they are exceptional thinkers who have changed their perspectives. Before they became wealthy, they learned to think wealthy. You might think of money in terms of the number of hours it takes you to earn it, the pennies and dimes you can save by couponing and flipping satellite plans, or your modestly rising savings account. Millionaires, on the other hand, see the capital in terms of concepts. It's not like it's a scarce resource that needs to be hoarded. Rather, it is the product of putting positive ideas into reality. They realize that to make a lot of money, they must use both ingenuity and leverage. Millionaires know how to think wealthy, and they know how to act rich because they know how to think rich. Acting wealthy entails more than cruising around in a limo and impressing your friends and colleagues with your Armani suit range. It's about treating people with the same dignity and compassion that you want to be treated with. It leads an active lifestyle, constantly on the lookout for new investment opportunities or business ventures. Continue reading if you want to learn more about millionaire psychology and how to think rich. It will show you how to supplant your negative idea designs to consider yourself a millionaire quantifiable. You'll find useful information in this section, such as:

Negative views about money that limit you.

Identifying a mentor.

Putting the best foot forward to excel.

Concentrating on making money.

View money in a nonlinear manner

There's a lot more. Best wishes to you as you work to improve your way of thinking and reap the rewards in terms of financial success

Take After Them

Many of us have limiting beliefs about income, hard work, and success, to name a few. Millionaires are distinguished from the rest of us by their resources and how they think. This mentality encompasses not just how they think about money but also how they think about themselves, their surroundings, and life in general. In other words, they have a mentality that prefers success over mediocrity or survival.

They have a good outlook on life

We've all heard about the importance of thinking positively. Negative words, such as "I don't want to eat spaghetti for supper," can be turned into "I want to eat a hamburger for supper." This upbeat attitude isn't just a way to get through a bad day; it's also one of the keys to millionaire thought. Money has a lot of negative connotations. You've most likely seen a lot of them. Here are a few examples:

- You can't buy happiness with money.

- Money is the cause of all evil.

- A person who wants a large amount of money is selfish.

- Money and wealth can contribute to feelings of loneliness, alienation, and misery; look at how disappointed lottery winners are.

If most millionaires believed these sayings, they would not strive as hard to achieve their goals. Rather than depending on these hypotheses to explain your lack of resources, consider changing your attitude. Change your mindset about money, achievement, and prosperity from negative to positive affirmations about yourself and the world.

- I already have everything I need to develop into the person I want to be.

- I have the imagination and work ethic necessary to achieve the prosperity I desire.

- I can amass wealth and capital.
- Rather than being in debt, I will live in luxury and prosperity.
- I am capable of being the good person I imagine myself to be.

Practicing the art of appreciation and thankfulness for what you already have is even better.

- I am grateful for my home and the people that surround me.
- I am grateful for my income and work.
- I am grateful that I can save money.

It may substitute these claims for those that refer to your own life and circumstances. Just remember to check all negativity and moaning at the door and concentrate on the better.

Mentors are available to them

The majority of millionaires did not become affluent on their own. Rather, they sought out people whose lifestyles they respected and imitated their behavior. To put it another way, they sought mentors. Mentors are people who have been there and done that before. They've already made blunders and crossed boundaries. Although their success will not translate to your success, they will be able to demonstrate what works and what does not. You don't have to fail in the same ways that others have struggled on the path to financial success and prosperity. It will help if you discover somebody who can show you how to be more compelling and settle on better financial decisions.

Try Success On For Size

If you had become a millionaire, how would you proceed? I'm not referring to the things you'd purchase or the home you'd move in. I'm referring to the day-to-day decisions you make, especially how you communicate with others and with yourself. Make those decisions right now. The disparity between how people view you and how you perceive yourself will astound you.

Will you change your outfit? Perhaps you fantasize about wearing an Armani suit every day. Maybe you'd put your hair up in a nice way and wear makeup and jewelry every day. Begin doing those stuff right now. You may not support the expense of an Armani suit, but it is a dumb decision to purchase one. However, begin dressing for performance. Wear a sports jacket and tie. You should get up 10 minutes earlier than normal to do your hair and makeup. Dress and show yourself as if you have the potential to be a millionaire.

If you were a millionaire, how might you treat others? Are you willing to be more generous? It is pointless to put off being compassionate and kind to others. You may not be able to donate $50,000 to charity right now, but you may be able to give $50 or volunteer elsewhere. It would help if you generously tipped the waiter or waitress.

How would you handle yourself if you unexpectedly became a millionaire? If you have a lot of negative self-talk — if you wouldn't talk to your best friend or family members how you talk to yourself — you might imagine talking to yourself and seeing yourself differently. Don't wait until you've amassed a large amount of money to see yourself in a new light. Strong affirmations about yourself and your talents should take the place of negative self-talk.

Some people's perceptions of you will change if you change how you view yourself and the people around you. When people see you arrive at a job beautifully dressed and polished every day, when friends and family see you treat others and yourself with respect, you are becoming a millionaire when you see you as a kind and loving person.

✦ They concentrate on making money.

If you're like most middle-class Americans, you probably think of your income as being small (you may get a Christmas bonus and a yearly raise, but for the most part, you are stuck at a certain earning level). You're probably still searching for ways to hoard and save money in the event of a tragic event such as a work loss or serious illness. You may be searching for small ways to save money, such as spending hours per month looking for coupons or switching to a $10 cheaper phone plan. Although living within your means is a worthy goal, this hoarding mentality would prevent you from achieving true wealth through a millionaire mindset.

When it comes to money, millionaires think differently than the rest of us. Instead of concentrating on how to increase their wealth, they concentrate on how to increase their profits. Of course, they know the importance of setting money back. They are, however, less concerned with small profits, such as a 1% interest rate on a savings account, than with discovering where big money is hidden. Rather than putting all of their money in a savings account, they may decide to invest it in the stock market or a business venture, giving it the potential to grow even faster. Rather than concentrating their mental resources on living as frugally as possible, they seek novel ways to make large sums of money.

They are well-versed in the use of leverage

Most people in the middle class appreciate the importance of hard work. They go to work every day, rarely missing a day unless necessary, and work until they can return home. They should be proud of their paycheck because it is money that they have gained. They might not have had to work very hard for it, particularly if they work in an air-conditioned office, but they did.

Although millionaires recognize the importance of hard work, they also recognize the importance of leverage. Leverage is the process of maximizing results in all areas by using your tools, contacts, and network, as well as your time. If a part of your company isn't producing, prune it or use your network to find a way to make it profitable. Concentrate your energies on what works best to make the most of it.

Keep in mind that using people to get what you want is not the same as using leverage. Although some millionaires certainly hire people, this is a technique for cultivating enemies and alienating people to be inaccessible when you need their services. When you're leveraging people, always look for ways to give back to them and show them that you're not just trying to take advantage of them.

They do not consider money and time to be interchangeable

If you're like most middle-class people, the amount of money you make is almost definitely equal to the number of hours you work. And if you work for a salary rather than an hourly wage, you won't make any more money at work unless you put in more hours, unless you get promotions and bonuses. This model produces a linear view of money in which the sum of money you make is effectively fixed without putting in a substantial amount of extra time. Millionaires do not associate money, especially large amounts of money, with time. They realize that rather than working more hours, the best financial choices can be made by ingenuity and problem-solving — stuff that doesn't happen on a 9-5 schedule. The measure of money you can acquire is restricted simply by your creative mind and resourcefulness. A good idea implemented at the right moment can transform into a fortune almost overnight. Think of money in exponential terms, where ideas can produce infinite wealth, rather than linear terms, where time and money are directly associated.

✚ They have an action-oriented mindset.

Many middle-class Americans who aspire to be wealthy are, at best, taking inactive steps toward financial prosperity. They might be purchasing lottery tickets or sending resumes for a better career, one for which they may not be eligible. So they can only hope and pray that success will find them one day. Millionaires, on the other hand, are still searching for new ways to get involved. Rather than purchasing lottery tickets, they are searching for better investment opportunities. Instead of searching for better and better jobs, they are looking for lucrative business opportunities. Millionaires aren't waiting for a hero to come to their rescue and make them rich. Instead, they understand that their fortune is in their hands and that if financial success is to be theirs, they must be their heroes. They behave and assume responsibility for their decisions. They are still going forward and searching for fresh and groundbreaking ideas.

✚ Visions of the Future

Many of us are so preoccupied with getting through our daily lives that we don't think about what we'll eat for supper, much less where we want to be in five or even ten years. Sure, we can fantasize about the future. We may fantasize about getting married, purchasing a home, having children, obtaining a better job, returning to school, relocating to a larger city, establishing roots on a farm, or any number of other items. However, the number of people who work to make their idealized future reality is remarkably small.

Many people wish for the "good old days" to come back. They're so engrossed in nostalgia and longing for life to be the way it used to be that they can't make any plans for the future, and their visions are confined to how they think life used to be. They may feel that their best days are behind them, and they will spend the rest of their lives trying to relive the glory days. People who think like this will never be rich. Furthermore, they often become lonely and depressed as a result of life's bleak and gloomy outlook.

The millionaire mentality involves fantasizing about and saving for the future. Millionaires are still dreaming about how they want their lives to work out. They don't just fantasize about what they want out of life; they plan to make those fantasies a reality. They set financial targets and plan how to achieve them. Perhaps taking courses, learning a new skill, or hiring more employees would be needed to meet those objectives. It would then take those steps.

Millionaires understand that their best days are ahead of them rather than behind them. How do they know that the best days of their lives are ahead of them? And they work to make the future a better place than the past. Even if the past was good, the future has the potential to be even better. While looking backward in time can lead to sadness and isolation, moving ahead and looking to the future can lead to the hope that defines the millionaire mentality.

One's expectations determine success. Millionaires hope to make money and, most importantly, for their money to make money for them. They make choices to make more money, whether it's through new investment, a new business, or even a creative venture.

These action-based decisions aren't taken on the spur of the moment. Rather, they are the product of intensive thought processes that aided in their growth into effective individuals. Millionaires don't think negatively, and they don't think about themselves negatively. They don't consider money to be a bad thing; rather, they consider poverty to be a bad thing.

It takes time to cultivate a millionaire mentality. Undoing some of the negative thinking patterns, deciding to show your best self every day, and living an action-oriented lifestyle can take years of effort. The benefits, on the other hand, would undoubtedly pay off.

CONCLUSION

According to my knowledge, there are three essential components to consistently profiting in the markets. <u>They are as follows:</u>

1) A solid, time-tested methodology in which the trader has faith that it will provide an edge

2) A tailored trading strategy that is objective and in line with the Edge (and not the guitarist)

3) A Mindset That Is Positive, Realistic, and Fearless

All three are critical. If you only have one or two, you will not achieve the desired consistency. The key point is that none of the three are on the same 'level,' for lack of a better term. Allow me to explain.

I came up with the metaphor of a bicycle to describe this. Consider the front tire to be the Edge and the back tire to be the Plan. You now have a fantastic-looking bike. The third component, your mindset, is the actual movement or motion of the bike moving forward - that is, you are on that bike and providing the energy to propel it forward.

Please allow me to explain. A beautiful, shiny new bike sitting in your garage is useless unless you get on it and ride it, which is the purpose of a bike. As a result, there is an interdependence here. You can have a bike (Method and Plan), but that doesn't guarantee you'll get anywhere. All of this means is that you own a bicycle.

However, for you to get on and ride that bike (Mindset), the bike must exist (Method and Plan). So, if you have a Positive, Realistic, and Fearless Mindset, it follows that you must have a Sound Method and a Sound Plan, or you will not have the right mindset. Without the other two, it is impossible to have the right mindset.

Because any moron with a negative mental attitude can get on a deathtrap for a bike and ride off to financial disaster in this game, we call trading and investing.

As a result, it is critical that developing the proper mindset is at the top of your priority list. It should be front and center. You can work on it concurrently with your Method and Plan, as well as as you gain market experience.

You can use the most sound methods and still lose money if you don't have a winning attitude and the right mindset. Why is this so? Because if your mindset is off, you will find a way to sabotage even the soundest investment strategies and plans.

When you observe a winner's attitude, you will notice a rock-solid level of confidence and certainty. Most people believe that winners are self-assured and certain because they win. That is not correct.

Winners consistently win because they are confident in their abilities. No matter how sound or unique, no method will work for any trader who imagines themselves losing. We must select a winning mindset.

You can never fail unless you permit yourself to do so. You can't feel like a loser or a failure unless you permit yourself. Nothing, no one, and no trade can make you feel anything. No market maker, talking head, politician, spouse, enemy, or friend can manipulate your emotions in any way. You make decisions, albeit most of the time subconsciously, but you do make decisions.

With each day, all you are experiencing is an experience itself, and you can choose to label it as a loss, a failure, an error, a lucky win, or a blunder, but why not call it a stepping stone to trading mastery'? Or is it another step toward your goals? Recognize that achieving any goal is simply a matter of taking action, monitoring the results, and then taking corrective actions to move you closer to your goal.

www.ingramcontent.com/pod-product-compliance
Lightning Source LLC
Chambersburg PA
CBHW081821200326
41597CB00023B/4334